FOREWORD BY REV. STEVE MENSAH

# TAKING TOTAL DOMINION

## BRIGHT BOATENG

# Reviews

To totally dominate in life one needs to overcome fear and live with a sound mind and courage. This book will give you step to step procedures as to how to experience your destiny.

**Dr. Kwaku Frimpong**
[C.E.O of Champion Groups of Companies]

With such a marvelous life coaching material in your hands you are poised to take dominion in both the physical and the spiritual realms

**Bishop Harrison Amoateng**
[Life Community Church]

We are born to dominate situations. This book reminds and occupies you with the right mindset to overcome challenges based on the word of God. Be inspired as you this book.

**Kwaku Owusu Boateng (Student)**
[University of South Australia, Australia]

# Dedication

This book is dedicated to the Holy Spirit who is my source of strength, comfort and knowledge of God. Again, this book is dedicated to my parents, Mr. Alexander Sampson Kwadwo Boateng and Mrs. Sarah Konadu Boateng and all my siblings for their love and support.

Finally, I dedicate this book to all readers who desire to occupy their dominion seats in Christ Jesus.

So he called ten of his servants, gave to them ten minas, and said to them *"occupy till I come." [Luke 1.9:13]*

Remember you are not born again, but to dominate again.

# Acknowledgment

First, I thank my heavenly father for the unquenchable hunger, and the quest for wisdom He has placed in me, the calling, and His anointing upon my life. I am grateful He would rather have me do His work than any other work on earth.

This work would not have been a success without the invaluable contributions of some very special people who made this book a possibility.

First and foremost, my sincere gratitude goes to Rev. Emmanuel Anning (Fountain House Chapel, UK), Apostle Dr. Kwaku Frimpong (Director, Champions Groups of Companies), Archbishop Prince Henry Hampel (Liberty Global Church), and Dr. Owusu Kwaku Boateng (Australia).

Thanks to Lawyer Benedicta Johnson of (Law Reform Commission, Accra - Ghana)

Special thanks goes to Mr Kofi Appiagyei for editing this book, may God richly bless you Sir. May the Most High bless and keep you all.

# Contents


Dedication...................................................................v

Acknowledgement.....................................................vi

Foreword.................................................................ix

Prologue..................................................................xi


Chapter 1: **Understanding Dominion**.....................1

Chapter 2: **Discovering Your Place Of Dominion**....7

Chapter 3: **Taking The Form Of God**.....................21

Chapter 4: **Possibilities Of Faith**..........................31

Chapter 5: **Possessing Dominion Mentality**............43

Chapter 6: **Creating Productive Atmosphere**.........67

Chapter 7: **Upon Your Confession**.........................91

Chapter 8: **What Am I Hearing?**............................103

Chapter 9: **Dominion Is Your Birthright**................113

Chapter 10: **Prayers Position You Well**..................123


Other Books By The Author.....................................138

About The Author...................................................139

# Foreword

In recent times, there has been a radical emphasis on faith which empowers one to walk in dominion the emphasis being on the study of the word of God. In order to be dominion-minded, individuals must increase along with their quality of prayer.

I am one of those who believe in seeing yourself as God sees you. I liberally love by faith, exercising the dominion mentality. This I have done for many years now without which I would not have reached this far in my ministry to the Lord and man. God mandates us to walk in dominion.

I can say here that this book by Pastor Bright is yet another arrow God has given to his children with which they can fight a good fight and exert their authority and dominion on this earth.

As you read page after page of this wonderful book, you'll realize that Pastor Bright will be taking you on a rather interesting spiritual journey; a profitable one too. He brings to life every point he makes.

If you want to renew your mind positively, you have the guidebook you need in your hands. You will not read far before you realize you are absorbing some very good teaching on having dominion.

Be blessed as you read on.

**Rev. Steve Mensah**
Senior Pastor
Charismatic Evangelistic Ministry
Accra

# Prologue

The world is full of struggles, challenges, and competitions. This is as a result of the fallen state of man and our inability to occupy our place of dominion; the position that God pre-ordained for us before man was created. People are being challenged by situations and circumstances to take their position and the ignorant are also competing for what they ought not to compete for. This has created a lot of chaos, disorder, and confusion in the world. People are killing others for position, money, and fame. Satan has denied people of their position, strength, blessing, and all other good things in life because they are ignorant about the fact that we are born and called to dominate.

From the genesis of creation, God had in mind that He will create man to dominate His other creations. This was to be done in the form of stewardship by God's grace. That means man's power to dominate was to come from God.

God delegated authority to man to have dominion over his other creations on earth.

Man ought not to struggle to discharge God's program because He who has all power gives us authority to discharge His program on earth to his glory. God is omnipotent and the owner of all things *"The earth is the Lord's and the fullness thereof, the world and they that dwell therein"* [Psalm 24:1]

Again, God gives us the requisite power to overcome any challenge that comes our way in order to fulfill our destiny's mandate. Challenges will surface in the pursuit of your destiny, but the grace you have received from God to surmount and triumph over them is more than enough.

Lastly, man was not born to compete, but rather to fulfill his destiny. You have your destiny to fulfill on earth. We should not compete with others because the authority given to us by God to fulfill His program is the same according to the Bible *"..., let us make man in our image, according to Our likeness; let them have dominion over the fish of the sea, over the birds of the air, and over the cattle, over all the earth, over every creeping thing that creeps on the earth."* [Genesis1:26]

The word "man" in the above scripture is the Hebrew word "Adam" which means, "that which is taken from the red earth" (on an individual or the species, mankind, etc). The above scripture can be paraphrased as, "let us make human being/mankind in our image, according to our likeness." All human beings are made in the image of God according to God's likeness. The phrase "let them have dominion" is for all mankind. "Mankind should have dominion over my creatures", said God. The same delegated authority from one same God.

Until one takes dominion, he or she will be dominated by money and all the other things one is supposed to dominate, it's very simple. Either you are dominating or you are being dominated by the sinful world. Arise as you travel with me in this book and get acquainted with the knowledge as you apply the principles in this book, dominion will be your portion. Read with joy and your life will never be the same.

***"You Cannot  Have God, (The Creator)," And Beg Men, (The Creature)"***

# CHAPTER 1

# UNDERSTANDING DOMINION

*"And God said, let us make man in our image, after our likeness: and let them have dominion over..."*

*[Genesis 1:26]*

The above scripture portrays the very intention for which God created mankind. The word "dominion' was voiced out by Jehovah God Himself even before the creation of mankind after He had created the heavens and earth. The Cambridge International Dictionary of English defines dominion as having control over a country or people or the land that belongs to a ruler. The word "dominion" appears in the King James Version of the Bible fifty-nine times. Considering the contextual meaning of the above text, the word "dominion" has several meanings. I would like us to consider the contextual meaning of the word "dominion, in the book of Genesis 1:26 because it was the first time the word "dominion" was used in the Bible.

The Old Testament was first written in the Hebrew Language. The Hebrew word for the word "dominion" is radah, (raw-daw), meaning to tread down, i.e. subjugate: to crumble off: (come to, make to) have dominion, prevail against, reign, (bear, make to) rule over.

For your information, the word dominion is a military word. If one carefully looks into the above definitions of the word in question, the words involved portray that something must exist for one to dominate it otherwise dominion cannot be in place.

Basically, two words come into play when the word "dominion" is mentioned. They are domain and dominate. To dominate is to have total control over a place or a person, or be the most important person or thing. The other word "domain" has to do with, 'a geographical area of interest or an area of which a person has control' (Cambridge International Dictionary of English).

Anybody who is willing to dominate must, first of all, discover his or her abilities (potentials), and also his or her domain (area/field) where he or she feels he or she can function well. Two things must be noticed here, these two have to do with your power/ abilities/capabilities, and place (a geographical area where you can be fruitful or function well). A geographical area where one can perform well is considered one's domain.

In the above definitions, certain words are sensitive and

are to be noticed if we are to properly understand the word, "dominion." We see the word 'subjugate' which has to do with defeat by completely controlling a group of people. Thus, to defeat people or a country and rule them in a way that allows them no freedom. Remember, no one can have victory, or defeat someone without fighting. The other word "prevail" means, to exist and be accepted among a large number of people, or to get a position of control and influence. The word 'rule' which also appeared means, 'to control, or to be the person in charge of (a country). Furthermore, the word reign also means to be king or queen in a country or to be the most noticeable or most powerful person or a thing in a place.

The most powerful and influential person in every kingdom is the king. The king is the decision-maker of the kingdom because he is the ruler in that domain. He makes sure that his decisions are implemented. He is the richest of the land, why? Because he is the owner and the controller of the land. All the resources are at his disposal. His wish is the command of the people of the land. Kings always subjugate, prevail, rule, and reign in their domain no matter what. Their words are final because it carries power *[See Ecclesiastes 8:4]*. The king can make and unmake as far as his jurisdiction or domain is concerned. Nobody can become a king on the same territory as long as the ruler is alive.

Every Christian has been called to dominate (tread down, i.e. subjugate: to crumble off :-(come to, make to) have dominion, prevail against or reign (bear, make to rule) over evil people, countries, something bad or diabolic circumstances. Christians basically, are the rulers of the land God gave to mankind because they have the spirit of Christ in them. Human beings, basically, have been born to dominate and rule over the other creatures on the land his creator gave to them. Men and Women who have a covenant with God through the blood of Jesus Christ have the delegated authority from God to rule over the earth till the rightful owner comes. *[See Luke 19:13]* This is because the earth is the Lord's and the fullness thereof. *[See Psalm 24:11]*. The owner of the earth is their father.

For your information, the earth is different from the world. Knowing the differences will help us to know how to live a victorious life. The earth is the tangible aspect of God's creation including what we see in the atmospheric heavens, whereas the world is intangible and a system that is governed by Satan, the prince of this world. In the beginning, God created the heavens and the earth and not the world (system). God was to govern the earth through mankind, His creature. That government is what we call theocracy. Theocracy is the situation where God rules through His servants. When Satan saw that God has given man authority to rule with Him and to dominate the earth, he came with a deception that man could rule and dominate without God, his creator.

After man had fallen through the disobedience of God's

instruction, Satan made man initiate a style of leadership and governance which is called the world. Now the Bible says, *"Satan is the prince of this world because he is the initiator of that kind of leadership."* *[John14:30]*

The earth is a place or geographical location where mankind lives whereas the world is a system of governance instituted by sinful men who operate their life. In fact, the world is the belief system of a group of people in a geographical area. Every geographical area has a group of people who live there with certain thought patterns and culture. This is why we do not have first or second or third earth, but we have the first to the third world. God did not create it that way. In the sight of God, there are no categories in governance. The word of God which should govern mankind has the same value everywhere.

The earth is the same everywhere, but the world varies from one place to another because it has different people who have different belief systems. The sun, the moon, the mountains, the sand, etc., can be found everywhere in the world. You have the power to dominate the earth, but you may not have to power to dominate the world (system). Those born of God or born again have been given the power to overcome the world (Satanic laws and leadership) *[See 3 John 5:4]*. To dominate the earth and to overcome the world (the system), one must be born again and be filled with the Spirit and the Word of God.

CHAPTER 2

# DISCOVERING YOUR PLACE OF DOMINION

For you to discover your rightful place (position) you must, first of all, know the place (position) you find yourself.

In life there are two places (reigns, positions), these are the existence place (position) and the living place, outside the presence of God and in the presence of God. Inside the Garden of Eden where God's presence saturates, is a perfect example of a living place, and outside the Garden of Eden where God sent Adam and his wife to live is also a good example of a place of survival or existence. Where you can live is your domain, and where you exist is outside your domain which is called a place of survival. You are either living or you are existing in a place. God wants you to live which means to have eternal life and not to exist which implies having a short life. *"And I said to your blood; live."* [Ezekiel 16:1-6]

To "exist" is to be under a very difficult condition or

with little food or money. When a person is at an existing place that person cannot enjoy life to its maximum. That person is not living in a good condition that will enable him or her to have the time to unearth, maximize, and utilize his or her potential to the benefit of others. In fact, an existing person ends up living under the mercy of others. Although he or she is alive, he is not living, he is just surviving. To exist is to just struggle whiles you are alive. A person who is very sick and cannot discharge his day-to-day duties is alive and existing, but not living.

To live is to be healthy in the body, spirit, in the mind, and, having all the things that pertain to life and Godliness at your disposal which will enable you to fulfill your purpose on earth. Having the power and the opportunity to do what you want to do in the pursuit of your God-given dream. In Eden, before sin came to the scene, Adam and his wife were living life to its maximum.

## YOUR PLACE(POSITION) OF DOMINION

In the world of soccer, every team has to provide eleven (11) players on the pitch for the game. Each of the eleven (11) players has a position to play and a certain role. We have the goalkeeper to keep to protect the ball from entering into the net, we have defenders also, the midfielder and the strikers.

The defenders may be three (3) or four (4) depending on the game plan of the technical coach. Among the three (3) or four (4) defenders, each defender has a specific position he or she is given. A defender may be good at the third position, another may also be good at the central defense, do you know that a defender who is good at position three (3) may not be able to play well as the central defender even though he or she is a defender? That means no soccer player can play well at all the positions, there is always a specific position every player can play well. No matter how good a player is he will be very good when they discover their rightful position on the pitch of play.

***"For in Him we live, and move and have our being,"***
[Acts 17:28]

Your location goes a long way to determine your achievement. Taking dominion is made possible when one is able to discover his or her place of dominion in life. Without one discovering his or her domain or place, he or she cannot dominate. For instance, a king cannot dominate any domain but his. Again, fishes cannot live and grow well outside water which is not their domain. They can only enjoy life in their domain which is water. Certain animals do well in the forest, some perform very well on the mountain top, others in the air or sky. Similarly then, everybody has a place in life where dominion is possible for them, and that place needs to be discovered. Until your place(position) of dominion is discovered you will live a substandard life. When God created mankind, He put them in a confined place (position).

*"And the LORD God planted a garden eastward in Eden; and there He put man whom He had formed."*

*[Genesis 2:8]*

The word, 'there' has to do with a specific place. The word, 'There' also has to do with somewhere and not everywhere. God put mankind somewhere that they could function well and flourish. From the onset, the all-knowing God put man in a conducive environment where he could make it and serve Him. The place where God placed mankind which was the presence of God, was an environment for productivity if mankind should engage in any activity. God did not just allow man to choose where he should be, but rather He chose a place for mankind. God could visit man because He knew the whereabouts of man whom He had created in His image and likeness.

When Adam and Eve dislocated from where they were destined to dwell which is the presence of God, they had a problem with their creator and therefore could not function well to their maximum. Mankind cannot function well if they have no good rapport with their creator.

*"And God called unto Adam, and. said unto him, where are you?"*

*(Genesis 3:9)*

The above question indicates that Adam displaced himself from his original place that is why God could not see him. Mankind got lost. To get lost in life is to leave the presence of the Almighty God. God purposely created us to live in Him because in Him is life. To get lost means one becomes unfamiliar with his current place and finds it difficult to go back to his rightful place. *[See John 1:4, Acts 17:28]*

So many people have lost their place in life and therefore they are in a confused state. Adam and his wife became confused the moment they left God's presence. This is the reason why they used leaves to cover their nakedness. Adam got lost, God used to visit him and man could perform his duties, but when man left his domain, he could not discharge his duties as he used to. Anytime you move from His domain, you cannot dominate unless you relocate to His presence. Anytime you move from your domain you cannot function well.

In order for Adam and his wife not to be enticed by the beauty of the forbidden tree, they were not supposed to get close to it or even take a look at it. From what the Bible says, the forbidden tree was somewhere in the middle of the Garden and not in front of them.

If they had not moved from their place to where the tree was, they wouldn't have been attracted to it. Sometimes people want to go close to sin instead of the place of worship. The lust of the eye and the flesh can entice you to sin. Do not tempt God, and do not tempt yourself. Do not go close to where you can easily be tempted. *[See Psalm 1:1]* Draw nearer to God and He will draw nearer to you. *[See James 4:5]* Do not draw nearer to sin. Do not give the Devil your attention so that he will not give you direction.

Remember, evil communications corrupt good manners. *[See 1 Corinthians 15:33]* Do not associate yourself with people whose words can entice you to sin.

## HOW TO REALISE YOUR DOMAIN OR PLACE IN LIFE

Every living creature has been designed to bear fruit in a specific geographical location. Sweet potato can be fruitful in a specific area. Dates are well grown in desert places. Aquatic animals perform well in water. No country has every resource. Every land has the seed it can accommodate. In the same vein, every human being can be productive in a specific endeavour at a certain place. Your domain is your area of interest or an area you have control of.

To locate your domain is to locate your talent and the environment which will facilitate its development and its utilization. In Christ is where you can discover and develop your potential. You should be diligent to unearth your talent. Again, you should do well to find out the environment that will be suitable for the development of the talent you have. Every seed or plant has an environment that will enhance its growth. No matter the potency of a seed, it needs a suitable environment that will facilitate its growth. In Christ, one can find such a suitable environment.

Your domain embodies all the things which will facilitate the attainment of the purpose for which God created you. In Christ, God has given us all things that pertain to life and godliness. *[See 1 Peter 1:3]*

When God created Adam and Eve, He put them in an environment where He knew that they could function to their maximum. Dear reader, after you've discovered yourself, you have to find out where you can easily work. Every one of us has where he or she can function well based on one's abilities, capabilities, and training one has undergone. People who have the competence to become medical doctors and have received training as Medical doctors can function well in the hospital.

Potentially trained teachers can function well in the classroom, farmers can function well on the farm, and footballers can function well on the football pitch because all the facilities they need are available at that place. Locate where you can function well in life. Before you locate where you can function to your maximum, you might have been trained.

## HOW TO DISCOVER YOUR TALENT (POTENTIAL)

- Find out what you can do easily.
- Find out what you can do naturally.
- Find out what you can do joyfully.
- Find out what you can do without motivation.
- Find out what you can learn without stress.

## TO DEVELOP YOUR TALENT (POWER)

- Find out the right tools.
- Find out the right place or training ground.
- Get a mentor or a coach.
- Put your ability into practice

## TO OCCUPY YOUR DOMAIN

- Go to the field of your endeavour.
- Create a good environment by surrounding yourself with the right people.
- Be consistent and persistent in whatever you do.
- Be excellent oriented.

## HOW TO KNOW YOUR RIGHTFUL DOMAIN

- In your domain you will have peace to work.
- In  your domain you will have provision.
- In your domain the environment will accommodate you to be established.
- In your domain you experience expansion.
- In your domain you are satisfied.
- In your domain you are fulfilled.

After you have discovered your place or domain in the kingdom of God, you have to occupy it till Jesus comes. You are made to discover and to occupy until your master comes.

The word occupy appeared in the entire Bible only two times. It appeared in the book of Ezekiel 27:9 and the book of Luke 19:13 and both have the same contextual meanings and have to do with work.

*"All the ships of the sea with their mariners were in thee to occupy thy merchandise."*

*[Ezekiel 27:9]*

The root meaning of the word "occupy" in the above scripture is to braid, i.e. intermix; technical, or technology. To traffic (as if by barter); also to give or to be security (as a kind of exchange):- engage, (inter) meddle (with), mingle (self), mortgage, occupy, give pledges, be (come, put in) surety, undertake.

Jesus Christ who is the all-knowing God told his disciples, *"occupy till I come" [See Luke 19:13]*. I would like us to also consider the contextual meaning of the word *"occupy"* as it was used by Jesus as compared to the book of Ezekiel 27:9 and why Jesus told his disciples to occupy till he comes.

The contextual meaning of the word as was used by our Lord Jesus is the Greek word "pragmateuomal" (pragmat-yoo-om-ahee) means to busy oneself with, i.e. to trade: - occupy. Occupy as was used by Jesus means "do business". Occupy till I come' means, be consistent in doing what God wants you to do till Jesus comes. What business should one do? The business here means, do what God wants you to do. Jesus told us his mind, "My meat is to do the will of God" (John 4: 34). The word "meat" in the above text basically means desire. The principal desire of Jesus Christ was to do the will of his father through the medium of the anointing.

*"How God anointed. Jesus of Nazareth with the Holy Ghost and with power: who went about doing good, and healing all that were oppressed of the devil; for God was with him"*

*[Acts 10:38]*

With the person of the Holy Ghost and God's power, Jesus was busy doing the work of God. You have to fulfill your assignment on earth through your God-given potential and the grace of Jesus on your life.

Occupy which means 'do business' according to the Greek word means one should not waste time but should get busy fulfilling his or her call. Based on the word "busy" we got the word business. Business is that which keeps you busy and gives you meaningful life all the time, whereas an occupation is that which occupies your time. Out of the word occupy emerged the word occupation. Occupy yourself and time with something meaningful. If you are not at your place you create a vacancy. Make sure you occupy a place in life. Make sure you are doing something meaningful to His glory.

## WHY YOU SHOULD OCCUPY TILL HE COMES

*"And the LORD God took the man, put him into the Garden of Eden to dress it and to keep it."*
*[Genesis 2:15]*

From the onset of creation, before sin came to the scene, the Almighty God designated man to dress and to keep what He gave to him. God did not give man whom he has delegated His power to dress and to keep the land a definite time, but indefinite time to live. Till Jesus returns, the earth has been delegated to man to care for or manage it.

In our world today, there is no property that does not belong to somebody, there is no land that does not belong to somebody and there is no place that is not being possessed by someone. Even human beings are being possessed by the spirit of God or an evil spirit. It is either you belong to God or you belong to Satan. This is why after you have discovered your place you need to dominate over there till He comes.

If you have been called as an evangelist, do the work of evangelist well till he comes. If you've been called in any area of occupation, do it well till he comes. You are the prince or princess in that territory. Do not give the devil a chance. Stay and dominate where you have been placed.

## TOOLS TO DRESS AND KEEP

Before God told man to dress and to keep what He had created, He had given him the power that would enable him to dress and to keep the land. God did not make a mistake by not giving him something. God gave them provision before he gave them an assignment. God gave them the ability to see, hear, taste, feel, and smell as basic gifts. He also gave them knowledge, understanding, wisdom, and various creative skills that will enable them to do what He intended them to do.

To dress means, "To till" and to keep means, "to protect". Where God stopped became the starting point of man that He had created in His image and likeness. You cannot do God's assignment without His anointing. Anyone who has received the power 'to dress' and the power 'to keep' is in charge and therefore is dominating. "Occupy till I come" (Luke 19:13) was a direct statement that proceeded out of the mouth of Jesus Christ when he was narrating a story that had to do with the kingdom of God. Jesus having knowledge of the devices of Satan, and knowing that he can take advantage of us told us to occupy our position till he comes. If we love God by serving Him with all our might, Satan cannot take advantage of us. Your might consists of your spirit, soul, and body.

It is written, ***"Whatever your hand finds to do, do it with all your might..."***

*[Eccl.9:10]*

Your totality should be given to God including your time. Satan takes advantage of people by stealing their minds and time, killing their faith, and destroying their relationship with God. Satan cannot get access to you if your attention is on God and His word. *"You shall meditate therein day and night." [Joshua 1:8]* It is only when you lose your focus on God that Satan can give you direction. When your relationship with God is distorted by the world's attractions, Satan will dominate you.

Why Jesus wants us to occupy till He comes is that if we fail to do what he wants us to do, we will end up doing what he doesn't want us to do. That means the devil will use us to do his will. If we don't allow the LORD Jesus Christ to ride on our talents, time, skills, resources, etc., Satan will ride on them to promote his course.

In the following chapters, we will consider some prerequisite principles that will enhance and facilitate our desire to take total dominion.

## PRINCIPLE OF TAKING DOMINION

On earth, you cannot succeed everywhere but somewhere. You cannot also succeed in everything but in something. You cannot succeed in every way but in some way. You cannot succeed with everybody but with somebody.

# CHAPTER 3

# TAKING THE FORM OF GOD

Before man can take total dominion in his domain, he must, first of all, take the form of God, his creator. God knows who we ought to be if we have to take total dominion over His creations. Then God said,

**"Let us make man in our image, according to our likeness; let them have dominion..."**

[Genesis 1:26]

When God said let us create man in our image, it means God has an image (representative figure) and our likeness 'also means God has a model so God created us in His own image and His own likeness. We need to find what God's image and likeness are if we have to reflect it. God's Image is His phantom which also means His spirit or ghost; it can also be a shade of Him. The image of God is the shadow (Spirit) of God and it never dies. God's spirit is always holy. God's likeness depicts love, cleanliness, dependability, flexibility, friendliness, humility, joy, orderliness, and kindness amongst others. We have looked at what God's image and likeness are even though we did not consider it in detail, but the few that we have considered should be noted very well. Taking the form of God is being in the image and the likeness of God. The word image in the book of Genesis 1:26 is the Hebrew word, "Tselem" (tseti-lem), derived from an unused root word which means shade, a Phantom of resemblance, or a representative figure. This means if we are to be in the image of God then we must resemble God and be a representative of God on earth. It also means we must be the shadow figure of God; an exact representative figure on earth.

**"In the image of God created him; male and female, he created them"**

[Genesis 1:27]

The above scripture makes us understand that God created man in His very image so that man can take dominion over the earth. That has been God's intention before man was created. After God had created man, man was given authority to fulfill God's preordained purpose. God commanded man to reign and rule on earth.

**"And God blessed them, and subdue it; have dominion over the fish of the sea, over the birds of the air: and over every living thing that moves on the earth"**

[Genesis 1:28]

Man's power was a delegated power. We were made to be stewards over the creations of God and expected to give an account of our stewardship.  Man named all the living creatures on earth according to Genesis 2:l9-20. Man was able to do 'these because he was in the image and likeness of God.

Likeness in the Hebrew word is 'demuwth' (dem-ooth) dew-maw, which means to be likened.

## THE FALL OF MAN

As I have already indicated, man was created in the very image and likeness of God his creator. Mankind could not die; Mankind was created to live indefinitely. Because God cannot die, His image (shadow/spirit) which is mankind also could not die. *[See Genesis 2:7]*

Being created in God's likeness, mankind was to love, to be holy, to be loyal, to be generous, to be creative, to be joyous, and to live in fruitfulness without dying. Mankind was created in that nature to be God's representative on earth, but something happened. Mankind who was to dominate nature through obedience and loyalty to God lost their position because they chose to obey Satan. This brought about the fall of man.

If we leave our state where God has created for us, we will surely succumb to the instructions of Satan and will automatically fall.  If we leave the place of holiness we will end up in the place of evil. If we leave the place of love we will end up in the arena of hatred and confusion.

**"Then the Lord God called to Adam and said to him, where are you?"**

*[Genesis 3:9]*

The above scripture bears the question of position. Man lost his position and the glory that goes with it due to sin. If I may ask, where are you, dear reader? Are you dominating and glorifying God?

Genesis 3:6 reads,
**"So when the woman saw that the tree was good for food, that it was pleasant to the eyes, and a tree desirable to make one wise, she took of its fruit and ate. She also gave to her husband with her and he ate"**

Sin always looks attractive and desirable at the initial stage, but in the end, it leads to death. Sin has the ability to allure you and lure you. The sin they committed was a sin of commission. Man knew the outcome of what he was doing because God told him previously.

## THE BEGINNING OF SUBJECTION
As soon as Adam and Eve sinned, they lost the glory of God which was upon them. Their sin affected the whole human race.

**"For all have sinned and fall short of the glory of God"**
[Romans 3:23]

Mankind's glory faded away when sin came on the scene. The blessing of parity and equality of mankind was destroyed. Racism, tribalism, manipulation, inequality, competition, struggling, and challenges started and the result of all these was death.

*"For the wages of sin is death..."*

[Romans 6:23]

Mankind could not take their dominion seat anymore, instead of ruling and reigning over animals, trees, and natural resources, tilling (dressing) the land and keeping it. *[See Genesis 2:15]* Man started fighting against his neighbour. Sin dominated the human race instead of the human race dominating sin.

## RESTORATION

When God saw what had happened to mankind; His very image, He decided to do something about the situation because His pre-ordained purpose was to be fulfilled. As aforementioned, mankind was created in God's image (spirit) therefore they could not die, yet because God had already told man that if he ate the fruit of the tree of knowledge of good and evil they would die and he did eat, mankind became subject to death.

*"But of the tree of the knowledge of good and evil you shall not;. eat, for in the day that you eat of it you shall surely die"*

[Genesis 2:17]

Mankind being dominated by death because of sin could no longer rule perpetually. For this reason, God had to send Jesus Christ to be reposition in Christ to rule and take dominion. Based on the immeasurable love of God, He sent Jesus Christ His only begotten to die for us so that anyone who will believe in Jesus and accept Him as the saviour will not die but live to dominate.

*"For God so loved the world, that whosoever believes in Him should not perish but have everlasting life."*
*[John 3:16]*

Whosoever accepts Jesus Christ as his Lord and personal saviour, Jesus comes to live in that person and the person takes back the very form of God. This gives the person a new life because the person takes on the very image of God as he accepts Jesus Christ *[See John 10:10b]*. Jesus Christ is God and when He is resident in you, you take His form (likeness) and the image (the spirit) of God. You take dominion over sin and death. It was for us to take total dominion that the son of man came so that He might destroy the works of the devil. *[See 1 John 3:8]* When you take Jesus Christ as your Lord and saviour, He comes to reside in you and communes with you. *[See Revelation 3:20]*

The death and the resurrection of Jesus Christ brought victory to us. It restored us to our dominion seat. We can dominate as we accept Jesus Christ as our Lord and saviour. *"But God, who is rich in mercy, because of His great love with which He loved us; even when we were dead in trespasses made us alive together with Christ and raised us up together, and made us sit together in the heavenly places in Christ Jesus." [Ephesians 2:4-6]*

If Christ is in heaven and He is also inside you, then know that you are in heaven with him.

**"Far above all principality and power and might and dominion and every name that is named, not only in this age but also in that which is to come."**

*[Ephesians 1:21]*

## REFORMATION

When we take the form of God, we are made in the very image and likeness of God in Christ Jesus. Being born again is being born of God. When a person takes Jesus Christ as his Lord and savior, he experiences a divine transformation in his life. This is what we call regeneration.

Regeneration is the secret act of God in which He imparts new spiritual life to us. This can only be done by God. We are regenerated by the grace of God which is the gift of God. It is the parents who give birth to children. We are born again by the grace of God and the power of God.

**"But as many as received him, to them He gave the right to become Children's of God, even to those who believe in His name"**

*[John 1:12]*

When one is born of God, he has been born to overcome (dominate) the world (system of governance instituted by sinful men)

**"For whatever is born of God overcomes the world"**

*[1 John 5:4a]*

The word overcome in the above scripture means to subdue, dominate, prevail over, conquer and get the victory. The person is born not only to subdue the earth but also the world. The world here means the philosophies and beliefs that are used to govern the earth; or the systems of leadership and governance instituted by sinful men. Because you are born of God (i.e. born again) you are imparted with the image and likeness of God to subdue the world (the system of sin). Being born of the word (Jesus) is being born to overcome the world (the system dominated by sin).

This is the first step in taking total dominion of the world (the system). You are saved.

**Power Quote:**

- When Jesus Christ rules over your life, you rule over principalities, powers, thrones and dominions.
- Where you position God in your heart determines where He positions you on earth.
- Life outside Christ is full of crisis and life inside Christ is full of calmness.

# CHAPTER 4

# POSSIBILITIES OF FAITH

In this chapter, we are going to learn one of the ways by which mankind can also dominate by exercising faith in God. The Holy Book reveals how we can please God who gives us the strength to dominate on the planet earth. For your information, if one does not please God, he or she cannot dominate. The Bible has stated clearly and categorically that without faith it is impossible to please God.

*"But without faith it is impossible to please God"*

*[Hebrews 11:6]*

Readers will agree with me that parents whose children do not please them, sometimes are reluctant to bless them and also feel disinclined or unwilling to discharge their responsibilities towards them. That means the child's behaviour is deviant to the parents. The child does what is contrary to the parents' instructions. This means the child displeases his parents. In the kingdom of God faith in Jesus Christ qualifies you to please God. If faith in Jesus Christ causes you to please God then let us find out what faith is.

Now, what is faith? Faith is to believe and behave (practising) what you believe with all certainty. So in Christendom faith can be defined as believing in God and behaving (practising) His word with all certainty or surety. If you believe it and do not practise it, it cannot be considered as faith. True faith is to believe and behave what you believe with all certainty. That is why the bible says

***"He who comes to God must believe that He is..."***

*[Hebrew 11:6b]*

The Bible uses the phrase *"must believe"*, implying that believing is a must and acting on that which you believe is also a must. One must believe in God and must act on his word without any iota of doubt and that is faith in God.

In dealing with the subject of faith, there are two types of it. We have the true faith and the false or untrue faith. The true faith leads to dominion and the false faith leads to slavery. The true faith is geared towards God through Jesus, but the false faith is geared towards other things and is always devoid of Jesus Christ. Faith in any other Being aside the Almighty God, the creator of the heavens and the earth is untrue faith or false faith. If anyone believes (exercises faith) in stone, trees, mountains, sun, stars, the sea, etc., that kind of faith is not the true faith. The true faith always believes and relies on (the one true eternal God) - God the Father, God the Son, and God the Holy Spirit. *[See 2 Cor. 13:14, Luke 1:35]*

Now for you to exhibit the true faith and please God your creator, you must recognize Jesus Christ as your Lord and saviour and accept Him and allow Him to be the Lord over your life. Walking in God's counsel with all your heart is faith which leads to dominion. Faith does not compromise the word of God but the total reliance on God's word. One of the characteristics of faith is obedience to the word of God. We see this in the life of Abraham.

***"By faith Abraham obeyed when he was called to go out to the place which he would afterward receive as an inheritance. And he went out, not knowing where he was going"***

*[Hebrews 11:8]*

Even though Abraham did not know where he was going, he embarked on that journey because he heard God speaking. A man of faith always stands for God no matter what.

In the book of Daniel chapter 3, we saw three Hebrew Christians who stood for God because they had faith in Him. There arose one wicked king called

Nebuchadnezzar. The king was very powerful to the extent that no one could disobey him and go unpunished. He made a declaration based on his decree that all the people in Babylon should bow down to worship his image. The decree was contrary to the beliefs of these three Hebrew young aliens called Shadrach, Meshach, and Abed-Nego.

The king pronounced to all the people living under his jurisdiction that as soon as the trumpet was blown in a particular ceremonial gathering, all the people should bow down and give reverence to his golden image which was his god. With all the power of the king and his authoritative rule, and even though these three young men were foreigners, they decided to stand firm to that which they believed because the decree of the king was contrary to their faith as God's people. Let us look critically at the pronouncement of that powerful authoritative wicked king and the end, the response of these three faith-filled Hebrew men.

*"Now if you are ready, at the time you hear the sound of the horn, flute, harp, lyre, and psaltery, in symphony with all kinds of music and you –fall down and worship the image which I have made good! But if you do not worship, you shall be cast immediately into the midst of a burning fiery furnace. And who is the god who will deliver you from my hand?"*

*"Shadrach, Mesharch, and Abed-Nego answered and*

*said to the king, O Nebuchadnezzar, we have no need to answer you in this matter. If that is the, case, our God whom we serve, is able to deliver us -from your' handy Oh king! But if not, let it be known to you, Oh king!' that we do not settle your' gods, nor will we worship the gold image which you have set up"*

*[Daniel 3:16-18]*

This response is very awesome and challenging. Even though the king promised to cast them into the fiery burning furnace, these three Hebrew young men did not deny their God. They decided to practise what they believed. What they believed was not to worship or bow down to any other god, except the Almighty God. They knew the commandments of their God which says,

*"You shall not bow down to them (gods). For Me, the Lord your God, am a jealous God...*

*[Exodus 20:5a]*

They had faith in God and they believed in His command, and practised the words or commandments of their maker even in the presence of the wicked king called Nebuchadnezzar. The true faith does not waiver.

It is said of Abraham that he staggered not at the promise of God through unbelief. *[See Romans 4:20]* Three Hebrew men did not waiver at the decree of the king. For your information, true faith does not doubt. *[See Mark 11:23]*

35

Doubting about the promises of God is not faith but rather fear. True faith is optimistic but fear is pessimistic. Faith in God is always real but not fiction. The reality of one's faith is the action the person takes as this action is the evidence of his faith, therefore, faith is a substance that always leads to hope - faith always walks hand in hand with hope. Faith is not always seeing. No one has seen God but by faith, we believe that He exists. *[See Hebrew 11: 6a]*

Jesus said to him,
**"Thomas, because you have seen me, you believed. Blessed are those who have not seen and yet have believed."**

[John 20:29]

The phrase 'seeing is believing' is not always true. There are things we must see to believe, but there are other things we don't need to see before we must believe *[See John 6:30]*. For instance God and the beginning of creation *[See Hebrew 11:3]*

No one has also seen germs with the naked eyes, yet we believe that they exist based on what they do. You can only see germs with a microscope so also you can't see God with your naked eyes, but we believe that He lives. We can only see God with the eyes of faith through Jesus Christ. Humanity's inner sense of the fact that God exists, the evidence of scripture and nature, the traditional "proofs" for the existence of God are among some of the proofs that God exists.

I want to use this opportunity to tell you that positive confession is not faith confession, neither is it faith. I don't depend on positive confession, but rather faith confession. What is positive confession? It is a humanistic pronouncement based on our natural conviction. Positive confession has no basis on the word of God. Positive confession is always selfish. It is sometimes fictitious or unrealistic.

For example, if I say I will like to fly by myself to another country without boarding an airplane to preserve my money, it is a positive confession, but it is unrealistic. Positive confessions say, I want to be a millionaire though I am a lazy person. I have seen a lot of lazy purposeless folks who are aiming to be on top by their positive confession. I have asked students in various schools who want to excel very well in their examinations to raise their hands. I saw both industrious and lazy students' hands lifted up. I asked one student whom I knew to be very lazy, why he thought that he would pass his examinations very well. He told me that his confession had always been positive and therefore it should come to pass. At the end of the day, this particular student failed.

Human words do not carry the power to make things happen, but God's word does. Human wishes are totally different from God's will.

*"For my thoughts are not your thoughts nor are your ways my way," says the LORD"*

*[Isaiah 55:8]*

One may ask, Man of God, if you consider positive confessions not to be the best, what confession do you want us to make because we know that words are powerful? Every serious Christian who wants to dominate must go for faith confessions instead of positive confessions which the Bible does not support.

What is a faith confession?  It is the consistent declaring or confessing the word of God as you believe it in your heart. If you believe the word of God in your heart and you confess it, it is faith.

*"But since we have the same spirit of faith according to what is written, I believed and therefore I spoken we also believe and therefore speak.*

*[2 Corinthians.4:13]*

Any confession which is outside the word of God no matter the excitement it brings to mankind is not a faith confession, but a positive confession. For example; if the word of God has not said you can fly like a bird and you confess and pray to God that He should grant you the ability to fly to wherever you want, even though you might be a Christian it will not be possible for you to fly because your prayer is outside God's word and therefore it is considered a positive confession.

Faith in God comes from the word of God; therefore knowledge of the word of God is the mother of faith. If you know and believe that God redeems, you will not be afraid in the midst of problems as a Christian. If you know and believe that God can and shall supply all your needs, you will not be scared in the midst of scarcity. If you know and believe by the word of God that you are the head and not the tail, you will always walk in dominion. If you know and believe as a Christian that you are above only and not beneath you will not undermine the word of God that said so. *[See Deuteronomy 28:12]* This kind of attitude makes God happy and He is pleased with you. This is why the Bible did not say, "The just shall exist by faith but rather it says, *"the just shall live by faith."* *[Habakkuk 2:4]*

You are made to live by faith, win by faith, overcome by faith, save by faith, enjoy by faith, etc., and not by sight. How can you have faith to please God? The Bible provides us the answer to that question.

**"So then faith comes by hearing, and hearing by the word of God".**

*[Romans 10:17]*

Aside from the word of God nothing gives and develops faith in God. The systems of the world will instill and develop fear in you, but The Word will give you faith in God.

## HOW FAITH GROWS

Faith grows in Christian living.  The more you hear the word of God and practise it, the more you see results and the more you see results, the more your faith grows. Based on this, one can say, the level of your knowledge of the word of God determines the height of your faith in God.  The book of Daniel chapter 11:32 says,

***"The people who know their God shall be strong and carry out great exploits"***

You cannot do exploits except you know Jehovah. The power of God only comes on you when you have realized your assignment and it increases in your life the more you increase your knowledge of Him.

## THE LORDSHIP OF CHRIST

The true knowledge of Jesus brings you to a place of total submission to God. If your Knowledge of the Bible does not let you submit to God's Lordship then it is not the true knowledge of God. Anyone who confesses he knows Christ will surely submit to God.  God is such that no one can complete His knowledge. You can know just a little knowledge of Him, but with your little knowledge of Him, you will still be overwhelmed by it which can bring you to a place of total submission. The total submission has something to do with obedience. God takes pleasure in you when you submit to Him because you acknowledge who He is. When this happens He brings you to a place where you take dominion. God endows you with what it takes to dominate in the Land of the living - when you allow him to dominate your life you also dominate on earth.

**Power Quote**

- Without faith it is impossible to please God
- You cannot be full of faith without being fruitful
- You can't exercise faith in God and fail, fall or fade away.
- You cannot have faith in God and be confused in the world.
- The level of your faith in God determines your outcome in life

# CHAPTER 5

# POSSESSING DOMINION MENTALITY

The mind of a man controls his body. It is scientifically proven that the mind is the center of the whole body of man. The place of decision making is the mind. Whether a good or bad decision it is the mind that determines it. Decisions lead to actions and every action has an outcome. The outcome will either be good or bad. Good outcome based on decision determined by the mind leads to progress, increment, longevity, and success and vice versa. The mind takes a decision based on the information at hand.

There is a way by which one develops his or her mind to be dominion-minded. If that way is ignored the mind will be affected negatively and the whole body will end in a mess.

**The Philosophy of Man**
What is philosophy? The word philosophy is two words joined together. It is the word

"philo" and the word "osophy". Philo means love and osophy means knowledge. So the word philosophy means the knowledge you love to study or memorize and practise.

Every human being on the surface of the earth, being a white man or black man, tall man or short, literate or illiterate has his own philosophy or belief. The philosophies we have are based on the information we have accumulated. The mind is a vacuum when we are born, it has nothing in it and therefore it is always empty at birth.

**The Concept of Mind Development**
The first place we start developing our minds is at home. Our parents are the first people who develop our philosophy. The information they have is transferred to us as they nurture us, so therefore their philosophy is likely to be transferred to us.

If a child is born into a traditional family, the child is likely to become a traditionalist. When the parents pour libation, the words they say get into the ears of the child and the child learns them. The child then comes to believe what his or her parents believe and practise. The child gets introduced to the practices of the parents deliberately or inadvertently from the beginning. If you begin to teach a child how to talk with insults, as we see in various homes in our part of the world, the child comes to believe that insults are normal.

Again, in a Christian home, when a child is born he or she comes to believe what his parents practise. The child may be born again, but he will come to believe the philosophies of his first teachers (i.e. parents). Also, when a child is born into Islam because of the education the child receives from his Moslem parents, he tends to develop a belief that has something to do with Islam.

The three scenarios above are true. This is because the mind is a vacuum at birth and whatsoever is put into it, is accepted. When a child goes to school in the formative years, he or she tends to accept whatever he or she is taught.

At the Senior High School, sometimes a majority of them have no idea about the courses to be tackled, this is because when they leave Junior High School, they go to Senior High School to study various courses. Some go for pure science, some for Business, some for General Arts while others study Visual Arts. Before the end of the first term, these four categories of students begin to develop an interest in their course. Sometimes, Business students don't understand what the Pure Science students say when they use their intimidating lexicon.

In like manner, visual arts students may not understand the terminologies of the General Art students. Though they may all have come from the same school, they have now developed their minds in diverse ways.

I have observed one thing, people from different geographical locations have different philosophies. It is not because they don't live in the same geographical area, but it is because they received different information and these have informed their philosophies regarding specific issues.

A Ghanaian born in the United States of America behaves like an American. Why is that so? It is because of the information he or she received where he was born and nurtured. I have seen an Australian man who behaves like a Ghanaian because he was born in Ghana and received his education in Ghana so he behaves like a black man even though he is a Whiteman. Irrespective of where people are born and bred, if they receive the same information and influence, they will have similar if not the same philosophy. Mental development is based on the kind of information and influence one receives.

The information you receive is much more important than your colour, height, or your ethnicity. The information you receive can either break you or build you. Inferiority or superiority complex is developed in us because of the information we receive.

Some people think that they are black people that is why they are poor; it is not true. The colour black is not synonymous with poverty. The fact that you are born black does not mean you should be poor. It is wrong information that leads to slavery.

## Philosophy Is Transferable

Do you know that philosophy is transferable? If you don't, I want to take this opportunity to let you know that philosophy is transferable. Jesus Christ knowing that philosophy is transferable decided to transfer His philosophies into us so that we can dominate over sin.

To begin with, Jesus who is the son of God and also God, foresaw that we have a wrong philosophy that has entangled us, making us slaves to the devil. Wrong philosophies should be aborted because it does not help one to dominate other creatures of God. Jesus being a lovely man in His time on earth saw that before He could impart his rich philosophies into us, He needed to do something that would cause us to abort our wrong beliefs which lead to sin. Let us consider the sayings of Jesus Christ our Lord who knows the best.

*"You have heard that it was said to those of old, 'you shall not murder', and whoever murders will be in danger of the judgment, but I say to you that whoever is angry with his brother without a cause shall be in danger of the judgment. And whoever says to his brother, 'Raca!', Shall be in danger of the council. (Sanhedrin). But whoever says, 'you fool!' Shall be in danger of hell fire. "*

*[Mathew 5:21-22]*

Jesus made the people aware that though their elders have told them that if anyone murders, he will be judged,

Jesus said their philosophy was wrong. Here, Jesus was trying to tell them that they should not think that it was only the act of murder that brought judgment upon one's head. That philosophy was of their elders' and should be aborted. The philosophy of Jesus is that even anger with one's brother will be subject to judgment. That is a good philosophy that Jesus imparts into His people (us) so that we can dominate.

If you are not angry with someone you will not murder him because anger leads to murder. This makes the philosophy of Jesus better than that of the elders. For your information, Jesus' philosophy is always better than any other beliefs of any group of people, culture, or tribe in the world.

## SOME PHILOSOPHIES OF JESUS

### Jesus abhors adultery;

*"You have heard that it was said to those of old, 'you shall not commit adultery' but I say to you that whoever looks at a women to lust for her has already committed adultery with her in his heart."*

*[Mathew 5:27-28]*

### Jesus is against divorce;

*Furthermore it has been said, 'whoever divorces his wife, let him give her certificate of divorce, 'but I say to you that whoever divorces his wife for any reason except sexual immorality cause her to commit adultery:*

*and whoever marries a woman who is divorced commits adultery.*

*[Mathew 5:31-32]*

## Jesus forbids oaths;

In Matthew 5:33-37, Jesus speaks to his disciples.

*Again you have heard that it was said to those of old, 'you shall not swear falsely, but shall perform your oats to the Lord.' But I say to you, do not swear at all: neither by heaven, for it is God's throne nor by the earth. for it is His footstool: nor by Jerusalem, For it is the city of the great king. Nor shall you swear by your head. because you cannot make one hair white or black. But let your 'Yes' be 'Yes' and your 'No' be 'No'. For whatever is more than these is from the evil one.*

Jesus portrays His philosophy here by saying in Matthew 5:38-42

*You have heard that it was said, "An eye for an eye and a tooth for a tooth; But I tell you not to resist an evil person, but whoever slaps you on your right cheek, turn the other to him also. if anyone wants to sue you and take away your tunic, let him have your cloak also. And whoever compels you to go one mile, go with him two. Give to him who asks you, and from him who wants to borrow from you do not turn away."*

## JESUS' PHILOSOPHY ABOUT LOVE

*"You have heard that it was said, you shall love your neighbor and hate your enemy.  But I say to you, love your enemies, bless those who curse you, do good to those who hate you and pray for those who Spitefully use you and persecute you., that you may be sons of your Father in heaven; for he makes his sun rise on the evil and on the good, and sends rain on the just and on the unjust. For if you love those who love you, what rewards have you?  Do not even the tax collectors do the same?*

*And if you greet your brethren only, what do you do more than others? Do not even the tax collectors do so? Therefore you shall be perfect just as your Father in heaven is perfect."*

*[Matthew 5:43-48]*

The philosophy of Jesus goes on and on.  If you look critically at the above scriptures, you will realize that Jesus Christ, first of all, quotes the beliefs and the philosophies of the elders and then continues by saying 'but I tell (say to you)'.

Here Jesus wanted His disciples to come to the realization of the philosophies and the practices of elders.  At the end of the day, He lets His disciples know that the philosophies and the practices of the elders are not good enough to save them. They therefore should learn and practise His (Jesus' philosophies). If what is in your mind is not good, your behaviour will follow the same pattern.  You only behave, practise or act on what you believe.

When Jesus came to earth, He started a school. In His school, He had a multitude of students, but only twelve of them were to be trained as leaders. They were fully committed students. Jesus called and educated them; He saw that these people already had a pattern of mentality. Based on the kind of information their leaders gave to them and the understanding they got, their mentality was formed in a specific pattern.

For example, they believed in loving their neighbours and hating their enemies, they paid evil for evil and good for good. They greeted their brethren and ignored their enemies. Jesus knew that these kinds of philosophies given to them by their elders made these people inferior to the standard of God's excellence, so He had changed them all by teaching His disciples the very true word of God.

The information given to them by their elders were not dominion kinds of philosophies that would have brought them to the place of dominion.  Jesus started to eradicate those kinds of inferior philosophies and inculcated in his disciples the dominion kind of philosophies. Jesus expunged the philosophy of the elders and taught His. In the end, the disciples learnt from Jesus and accepted Jesus' kind of philosophies. The impartation of Jesus Christ's new philosophies into the lives of His disciples was seen in their behaviour in the latter days. This made the People of Antioch name the disciples of Jesus Christ 'Christians' meaning, Christ-like because they saw them teaching and behaving like Christ their master. The disciples were first called Christians at the city of Antioch. *[See Acts 11: 26]*

## DEVELOPING DOMINION MENTALITY

As it has already been made clear, the mind is the center of the body. The mind controls, determined by the state of the mind. Thus to achieve a dominion mentality, first of all, one needs to work on his mind. If you win in your mind by the word of God, you will automatically win the battle externally. Internal victory produces external victory. That is why the bible says,

**"For as he thinks in his heart, so is he,"**

*[Proverbs 23:7]*

Anytime you think victory when embarking on something, you automatically win. Before coming to Jesus Christ and knowing God, the environment in which one is born inculcates in him both positive and negative philosophies. In order to develop the dominion mentality, one has to expunge the mind of all the' negative philosophies acquired along the line in his or her development. One can do this by recognizing that his or her philosophies are not in line with the word of God. He must abort that mindset by confessing how bad it is. He must try to learn the best and righteous philosophy which is the word of God. Learning begins when one accepts the fact that he is ignorant about what he thought was right. Those who think they know but do not know cannot be easily taught. We need to reject the mentality that has made us failures. Hatred mentality must be rejected and love must be developed for one another.

The Bible calls evil philosophies the works of the flesh because they only benefit the flesh, but do not strengthen the spirit of God in us.

*"Now the works of the flesh are evident, which are: adultery, fornication, uncleanliness, licentiousness, idolatry, sorcery, hatred, contentions, jealousies, outbursts of wrath" selfish, ambitions, dissensions, heresies, envy, murders, drunkenness, revelries, and the like; of which I tell you beforehand, just as I also told you in time past, that those who practise such things will not inherit the kingdom of God."*

*[Galatians 5:19-21]*

The Bible says those who practise such beliefs will not inherit the kingdom of God.

If you have been told to pay evil for evil, it is a wrong ideology; abort it. Some people go to their work places and instead of discharging their responsibilities diligently they ignore their task at work place and do their own things, at the end of the month, week or day they expect their remuneration to be paid. In some work places a group of lazy folks will discourage some hard-working colleagues by saying, 'do you own the company', or 'does the company belong to your parents? Don't kill yourself over this job, because the company is for the government.' This is a wrong perception. The truth is that you must be diligent.

**"See thou a man diligent in his business, he shall stand before great men and not mere men."**

[Proverbs 22:29]

## God's Kind Of Philosophy

The word of God is the mind of God revealed to us. The word of God is the Philosophy of God. It is the dominant philosophy a person can have (possess). Developing your mind with the word of God is developing the "dominion mentality". It is only the word of God that can bring us to the place of dominion when put to practise.

If all people tell you that you are a nonentity and therefore you cannot make it in life, God's philosophy which leads to dominion has this to say,

**"And the Lord will make you the head and not the tail; you shall be above only and not be beneath..."**

[Deuteronomy 28: 13]

If you feel intimidated and fear creeps over you, it is written of you,

*"For God has not given us a spirit of fear, but of power and of love and a sound mind"*

*[2 Timothy 1:7]*

Another word of God says, "Do not fear, little flock,.." *[See Luke 12: 32].* When you look through the eyes of God which is the word of God, we have three hundred and sixty five (365) "Do not fear" as statements written in the Bible.  That means, each day of your life God inculcates in the mind of his people through His word not to be afraid. If the philosophy of the world tells you that you will fail in life, and poverty will be your closest friend based on certain conditions; the philosophy of God or the word of God will resist it by saying,

*"Wealth and riches will be in your house..."*

*[Psalm 112 : 3]*

Beloved, I pray that you may prosper in all things and be in good health just as your soul prospers is what the word of God says in 3 John 2. When demons orchestrate to eliminate you from the surface of the earth, the philosophy of God says,

*"No weapon formed against you shall prosper, and every tongue which rises against you in judgment you shall condemn. This is the heritage of the servants of the Lord. And their righteousness is from me," says the Lord.*

*[Isaiah 54:17]*

Every area of your life has some words of God that will cause you to dominate in that area. You should fill your spirit and soul(mind) with the dominion word of Christ. If the word of God saturates your mind and spirit, dominion becomes your portion. The word of God is very powerful and it has the capacity to defeat every bad circumstance and also diabolic personalities that confront you. If you have the word of God, you don't fight for yourself, the word of God fights for you. The word of God gives you the wisdom to handle every evil situation thereby making you a champion. When you confront every situation with the word of God, that situation will give way.

The centurion sent some elders of the Jews to plead with Jesus to come and heal his servant and Jesus went with them. When Jesus was already not far from the house, the centurion sent friends to Him, saying to him,

*"Lord, do not trouble yourself for I am not worthy that you should enter under my roof. Therefore  I did not even think myself worthy to come to you but speak the word and my servant will be healed."*

*[Matthew 8:8]*

The centurion knew that the word of God carries power and when it is spoken, no matter the distance, something good will happen to his servant.

Jesus Christ had the word; which is the mind of God in Him. If both your heart and your mind is saturated with the philosophy (word) of God it flows out of your month naturally.

*"Brood of vipers! How can you, being evil speak good thing? For out of the abundance of the heart the mouth speaks. A good man out of the GOOD TREASURE of his heart brings forth good things, and an evil man out of the EVIL TREASURE brings forth evil things"*

*[Matthew 12:34]*

God told Joshua to develop a dominion mind.  He told him developing a dominion mindset is the only way by which he could be successful. God told Joshua how he could do that.

*"This Book of the Law shall not depart from your mouth but you shall meditate in it day and night. that you may observe to do according to all that is written in it. For then you will make your way prosperous and then you will have good success"*

*[Joshua 1:8]*

The philosophy of God should always proceed out of his mouth when he speaks.  He was urged to meditate on it day and night.  Meditation is done in the mind and in the heart.  He should also observe to do all that is written therein. The Bible says,  *"For THEN you will have good success; then you will make your way prosperous'.  The*

*Bible did not say, "Your ways, but your way."* That means you will only be on the way of prosperity. Prosperity has only one way. You only need to progress on the way of prosperity when you discover it.

The Bible also says *"good success"*. The word 'good' is an adjective that qualifies the noun success. That means one can also have bad success. It is God who makes us rich and adds no sorrow to it *[See Prov. 10:22]*. Success exempted from sorrow is a good success, but the success that goes with sorrow is a bad success.

A word (God's word) dominated minded person takes dominion of wherever he or she is.

**"Every place that the sole of your foot shall tread upon, I have given you as I said to Moses."**

*[Joshua 1:3]*

You are the one who can make your way prosperous by observing to do what is written in the Bible. *"For then you will make your way prosperous." [Joshua 1:8]* People whose minds and hearts are saturated with the word of God are always strong in every situation. People are not able to stand before them and win in battles. *[See Joshua 1:5]* They speak and people obey.

**THE POSITION OF THE WORD**
The word of God has 'three levels of positions'. Until you come to know this truth I am about to unfold, you

will continue to behave anyhow.  If one wants to define the word of God, it is simply Jesus.  And if one wants to find out who Jesus is, He is the word of God.

*"In the beginning was the Word. and the Word was with God, And the Word was God"*

*[John 1:1]*

Jesus Christ is the word of God and the word of God is Jesus. The word of God is manifested in Jesus.  Jesus Christ is the Word personified according to the revelation of Holy Scripture, let us consider this scripture.

*"And the Word became flesh and dwelt among us and we beheld his glory, the glory as of the only begotten of the Father, full of grace and truth."*

*[John 1:14]*

Now having known this, let us consider the three various positions of the word of God. Read the gospel of John Chapter 15:4-7, the Bible reveals the various positions of the word of God.

## FIRST POSITION, THE WORD IN YOU

*"If you abide in me, and" my words abide in you, you will ask what you desire, and it shall be done for you."*

*[John 15:7]*

The first position of the word of God as a Christian is the word in you. You cannot be in the word if the word is not in you. The word of God must settle in you if you are willing to dominate other than that, failure is inevitable in your life. It is only when the word of God is rooted in you that you can meditate on it day and night. You exhibit the word naturally when it dominates in your heart. If the word of God has told you that you are the head and not the tail and you begin to see yourself as the head and think as the head in faith, you become as it is written. *[See Proverbs 23:7]*

The information you receive everyday that has gained root in you is what reflects on your mind. If the word of God abides in you, you speak the word of God, think the word of God and practice the word of God.

Do you know that what you believe is how you behave and what you practice is what you become? You cannot deliberately practice what you don't believe. If one believes that doing good leads to divine blessing and grants one favour, one practices it willingly. Let the word of God settle in your heart fully and you will not be fooled, but you will be full of God's blessing. King David whom God loves said,

***"Your word have I hidden in my heart that I might not sin against you"***

*[Psalm 119: 11]*

60

To paraphrase what King David said, will be "Jesus have I hidden in my heart that I might not sin against God.

## SECOND POSITION, YOU IN THE WORD

The second position of the word of God is when the word of God which is in you is seen in you, it clothes you so much so that you cannot be seen.

"If you abide in me" in the book of John 15:7 are words from Jesus' mouth. What does it mean to abide in Christ who is the word personified? It means having total trust in the word, depending solely on the word. Living your life as it is written in the word of God. If the word says, "Be bold", be bold as it says. If it says, "Be humble, and you are humble, you are living and manifesting the word of God. People see the word of God in your day-to-day actions.

My dear reader, the word of God must engulf you so much so that you cannot be seen. If people look at you, they must see Jesus and not your attitude. You are hidden but Jesus is exposed in your life. *"He must increase but I must decrease"* said John the baptizer. [See John 3:30] Jesus should be known in your life and not you per se.

You are in Him means you are hidden in Jesus, but He is exposed in your life. Apostle Paul stated it in this way,

*"You are our epistle written in our hearts, known and read by all men; you are manifestly an epistle of Christ, ministered by us, written not with ink but by the spirit of the living God, not on tablets of the stone but on tablets of flesh, that is of the heart,"*

*[2 Corinthians 3: 2-3]*

If we are in the word of God, we are in Christ Jesus and our character should exhibit the nature of God who is resident in us. We will not find it difficult to preach Christ because we are ourselves the epistles that tell the world the mind of God.

## THIRD POSITION, THE WORD IN HEAVEN
*Forever, O Lord, your word is settled in heaven"*

*[Psalm 119:89]*

The third and final position of the word of God is in heaven. We have the first heaven, the second heaven, and the third heaven. The earth is only one, but the heavens are three categories.

*"In the beginning, God created the heavens and the earth."*

*[Genesis 1:1]*

Consider the following scriptures.
- *"For all the gods of the peoples are idols, but the Lord made the heavens"* [Chronicles 16:26]
- *"The heavens declare the glory of God..'[Ps. 19:1a]*

- *"Let the heavens declare His righteousness, for God himself is judge"* [Psalm 50:6]

The first heaven is the sky that we see. It is the atmospheric heaven. Then the sky receded as a scroll when it is rolled up..." *[See Revelation 6: 14a]* The first heaven is the same place where the sun, stars, moon, and the like are.

The second heaven is where some fallen angels dwell. It is inhabited by principalities, power, the rulers of darkness, spiritual host of wickedness and thrones. Apostle Paul says, *"They are in heavenly places."* *[Ephesians 6:12]* The satanic bodies fight men, resist their prayers, and cause those in authority to be proud and take evil decisions.

The third heaven is where God dwells. Jesus being God dwells in the third heaven far above principalities and powers who dwell in heavenly places. He came from the third heaven and He returned to the third heaven after His resurrection from the dead.

**"And while they looked steadfastly towards heaven as He went up, behold, two men stood by them in white apparel who also said, "Men of Galilee, why do you stand gazing up into Heaven? This same Jesus, who was taken up from you into heaven, will so come in like manner as you saw Him go into heaven."**

*[Acts 1:10-11]*

Jesus Christ being the word was taken to the third heaven by the power of God.  If we are in the word of God and the word of God is in us then where the word of God is, there we shall also be.

**"If then you were raised with Christ, seek those things which are above. where Christ is sitting at the right hand of God."**

*[Colossians 3:1]*

Now considering the above scriptures where are we now? We are where the word of God is. Our spiritual position is in the third heaven far above principalities, powers, dominions, and thrones, and they are far below us *[See Ephesians 1:21]* We rule with God In the third Heaven. We live above every situation and circumstance. The spiritual rules of heaven govern us. If the word of God fills your heart and mind, you take dominion on the things beneath you, including principalities and powers, poverty, sickness, and all those ill circumstances that are rampant on earth.

**Forever, O Lord your Jesus is settled in heaven. Forever, O Lord I am settled in heaven.**

## Power Quotes

- As a man thinks in his heart so is he.
- Guide your heart with all diligence for out of it are the issues of life.
- You are the product of your thoughts.
- It is not those who think positively that enter the kingdom of fulfillment, but rather those who do what they think.
- You cannot be faithful to the word and not being fruitful in the world.  Abraham became faithful to the word (God) and he became fruitful in the world in his generation.
- If you imagine good, good comes and if you imagine evil, evil comes.
- Your mind is the gateway to your destiny.
- Your thinking will either make you or mar you.
- The type and kind of information you have and acted on, determine the kind of transformation you receive.
- Your output is a product of your input.
- By the word of God heaven and earth were created and by the word the world was saved.
- You can't have the word and wander in the world. It is impossible.
- He that receives information from above is above all.
- If you are faithful to God you will be fruitful on earth.
- To be carnally minded is death, but to be spiritually minded is life and peace.

CHAPTER 6

# CREATING PRODUCTIVE ATMOSPHERE

The atmosphere you permit determines the attitude you convey. Life is about locations, and one's location will determine one's achievements. We have different kinds of locations and atmospheres. The whole earth is divided into seven continents. We have North and South America, Africa, Australia, Asia, Antarctica, and the European continent. These continents are divided into nations. Within the nations, we have cities, towns, and villages. It can also be called societies. In every society, we have a certain atmosphere.

Atmosphere constitutes the beliefs and practices of a specific area or locality. Every society has one kind of belief which may differ from another. In certain societies, the people believe that one should not eat a specific animal, such as a dog. Eating it, therefore, constitutes an abomination to them. Anybody who eats it is considered an odd person.

In another society what happens to a person concerns everybody. Therefore if a person dies everybody would like to know the cause of his or her death. In this kind of society, people talk about anything you. Whether good or bad, people will have something to say.

Also in some societies, the issue of one person does not concern another. You can do what you want if only it does not contradict the laws of that location. You can decide to sleep all day long, once it does not contradict the constitution, no one will talk about it. We also have a society that believes in practicing the extended family system. Anybody who relates to you either by blood, adoption, or marriage is said to be your family member and it is a must that you assist any of them when they are in need. This kind of practice has a lot of disadvantages. In fact, its demerits outweigh the merits. One can impregnate someone's daughter and it turns to become the problem of the whole family. One may be lazy and would not like to work to earn a living, he can misbehave and if it lands him in trouble, the whole family becomes responsible for it.

In some societies, hatred is or has become the order of the day. People naturally love to hate others especially, if one is progressing. They will do all that they can to stall one's progress. They fight each other so that others will not succeed. Those who are able to succeed look to demonic powers for protection. In such societies, people backbite a lot.

Considering the seven (7) continents in the world you can see that there are differences in each of them. Traditional differences, cultural differences, colour differences, etc. This is because of their beliefs, practices, and weather. The world itself is full of variations. That is how God made it.

## ATMOSPHERE

What is an atmosphere? The Oxford Advanced Learner's Dictionary defines atmosphere as "The feeling or mood that you have in a particular place or situation; a feeling between two people or in a group of people"

Now looking critically at the definition you can say, "An atmosphere is a state one has in a particular place or between groups of people." It can either be a good mood or a bad one. If you are in a bad type of atmosphere you are unable to make an impact. Your creative power will be suppressed and if your creative power is suppressed you can't produce and if you can't produce you can't gain and if you can't gain you can't dominate. Our gifts and talents die when we are in a bad place or location. People don't see your potency.

## TYPES OF ATMOSPHERE

In the book of Matthew, Jesus gave very classic examples of four different atmospheric places. Matthew 13:3-8, "Then He spoke many things to them in parables, saying: "Behold, a sower went out to sow; And as he sowed, some seed fell by the wayside: and the birds came and devoured them. Some fell on stony places, where they did not have much earth; they had no depth of earth. But when the sun was up they were scorched, and because they had no root they withered away. And some fell among thorns, and the thorns sprang up and choked them. But others fell on good ground and yield a crop; some a hundred fold, some sixty, some thirty."

## THE WAY SIDE ATMOSPHERE

This type of atmosphere is saturated with a lot of hostilities. In this atmosphere, people are ready to antagonize your greatness. The antagonists are there to make sure that you don't succeed. Your failure is their target. Their nature and attitude are like that of a serpent. The rivals mingle with you in a strategic manner so that you may not be able to recognize them as enemies. They have a secret diabolic agenda to fulfill in your life, this is the attitude of a serpent. These enemies come to fight you and to steal from you that which is the seed of your greatness.

When God created you, he put in you a seed that has the potency to make you great and dominate. That seed is so much so precious that it should be well protected. The enemies come with the intention of stealing, killing, or devouring it.

*"The thief does not come except to steal, and to kill, and to destroy,"*

*[John 10:10a]*

He uses human agents because he is a spirit and cannot handle physical things. When he comes around you, his mission is either to steal your seed of greatness or destroy it. You need to be very careful of the people who come around you. They may either be your friends or otherwise, do not just celebrate any person because he comes around you.  My Dear reader, people around you create your atmosphere so also do they soil the already created atmosphere for the seed.

## STONY TYPED ATMOSPHERE

This is another atmosphere that is very diabolic and deadly. It is diabolic and deadly because it is not conducive to physical and spiritual growth. It is hard to grow a seed on stony ground. You may succeed in planting it, but for it to grow and bear fruit is a big problem.  Jesus said, *"The seed started growing up, but due to the absence of soil (assistance) it could not stand."*  The root could not penetrate to gain grounds due to its stony nature.

In this type of atmosphere, there are no motivators. People are not ready to encourage you to move forward even though you are coming out with something good. They see the good things you are doing, but are not ready to support you with their money neither are they ready to encourage you with their words. Instead of people encouraging you by the word of God, prayer, or physical support which will lead you to the right contact, they will rather discourage you so that you don't achieve your goal.

If you find yourself in this environment you need to look up unto God where your help will come from. David found himself in such a situation when the people said, it is impossible for him to defeat Goliath. It came to pass that Israel had a face-to-face confrontation with Philistines. In this confrontation, the Philistines were defeating the Israelites. David who was sent by his father to deliver food to his brothers on the battlefield saw that his people were being defeated. He had the conviction that he could slay the giant who was leading the Philistines to defeat Israel. The champion of the Philistine was bragging (taunting) and spoke against the God of Israel.

***"Then as he talked with them, there was a champion, the Philistine of Gath, Goliath by name, coming up from the armies of the Philistine; and David heard them. And all the men of Israel, when they saw the man, fled from him and were dreadfully afraid."***

*[1 Samuel 17:23-24]*

All the Israelites hid because they were afraid of Goliath, the giant of the Philistines. David who was exempted from pusillanimity, (cowardice) decided to confront the giant. Let us take a look at what those people around him said,

***"Now Elias's anger was aroused. against David, and he said, "Why did you come down here? And with whom have you left those few sheep in the wilderness? I know your pride and the insolence of your heart. for***

*you have come down to see the battle. And David said, "What have I done now? Is there not a cause? "Then he turned from him toward another and said the same thing, and these people answered him as the first ones did."*

[1 Samuel 17:28-30]

David's immediate brother could not encourage him. What Eliab, the oldest brother said was the same thing the others said when he turned from Eliab to them. With the above scripture, I learnt that your own siblings or family members can be hostile to your dreams when you want to make progress. Now the actions of David were reported to the king who was the leader of the armies of Israel. Watch what the king said.

*"And Saul said to David, You are not able to go against this Philistine to fight with him: for you are but a youth and he is a man of war from his youth."*

[1 Samuel 17:33]

David had not gone to fight Goliath, the champion of the Philistines, but King Saul had already underestimated him. Remember, it is written,

*"Let no one despise your youth, but be an example to the believers in word, in conduct, in love, in spirit, in faith, in Purity."*

*[1 Timothy 4:12]*

My Dear reader, the way you see yourself is the same way people see you. You can be a pacesetter by example. Instead of David's brothers encouraging him for his acts of boldness so that he could push forward, they rather chose to discourage him.

Some people are not ready to go, but they will not allow you to go either. Some do not have the courage to do it, yet they turn to discourage you who aims at doing it. They envy you for the effort you are making and drag you backward with their mouth and other weapons. Some people are not creative, but they discourage your creativity. They curse you with their words spiritually and physically when you want to create something new. In this type of environment, you don't develop the deep root you need to survive there. They don't give you the backbone support. In this kind of environment, the probability of success is very low. Please do not stay there and struggle, relocate.

## THE THORNY ATMOSPHERE

This is an environment where people deliberately antagonize you. Here they literally fight your efforts. They are there purposely to make sure that you die destitute or your vision dies unfulfilled. Thorns can spring on a very potent plant till the plant gets destroyed. It chokes the plant, thereby making the plant weak and set for destruction. A perfect example of the thorny type atmosphere or environment is found in the book of Genesis Chapter 37:12 -36.

There arose a young man by name, Joseph. This young man had eleven siblings. He was the eleventh-born son. His father loved him more than all his brethren because he was the son of his old age. *[See Genesis 37:3]* This handsome young man foresaw that he would be a great person in the future. God had revealed to him that he would be a celebrated person in the future. *[See Genesis 37:6-77]* When he told his family about his dream (vision) instead of thanking God for such a wonderful revelation they rather envied and hated him. *[See Genesis 37:5]*

In fact, you need to be very careful whom you tell your dreams.

Some people can either hate you or love you for it. Joseph did not really know whom he revealed his secret to spiritually and mentally. His own brothers hated him already because he was loved by their father. As the Bible reveals, as soon as Joseph shared his dream with his own brothers they hated him the more *[See Genesis 37:5]*

An unconducive atmosphere was created for Joseph due to the fact that he told his own brothers his dreams. In order not to create a bad atmosphere of hatred for the fulfillment of your dreams, I caution you to be very circumspective of whom you share your dreams with even if you are bloodily related.

Joseph's brothers made up their minds to eliminate him. That was a thorny type of atmosphere that was created for him. They decided to harm Joseph physically when they saw him afar coming with their own food for their lunch.

*"Now when they saw him afar off, even before he came near them, they conspired against him to kill him."*

[Genesis 37:18]

They decided to do that because of what Joseph could become in the future. Your enemies directly and indirectly fight against you because of the seed of greatness in you. Their intention is to truncate the fulfillment of the vision you bear. Your enemies know that if the driver of the destiny, dream and vision dies, the destiny, dream, and vision cannot survive.

*"Come, therefore, let us now kill him and cast him into some pit; and we shall say, "some wild beast has devoured him. We shall see what will become of his dreams!"*

[Genesis 37:20]

The very reason you are facing that unpleasant atmosphere is that you are too loaded to be great and be a blessing to mankind that is why Satan is troubling you. Hook unto the anchor of life in the person of Jesus and you will fulfill your dreams and destiny. When Christ Jesus steps in, Satan steps out.

The young man David had the same experience as Joseph. David was a man of God endowed with so many gifts and had an unimaginable potential. David was so much talented that he was recognized by the people in the community. One day it came to pass that a distressing spirit troubled Saul the king of the land. King Saul gave orders to search for a man who is a skillful player on the harp to come and play and sing so that he could be delivered from his situation. They needed an anointed singer, not just a skillful player. *[See 1 Samuel 16:17-18]*

You may be skillful, but you need to be anointed in order to cast demons out.

***"Then one of the servants answered and said, "Look, I have seen a son of Jesse the Bethlehemite, who is skillful in playing, a mighty man of valor. A man of war, prudent in speech and a handsome person; and the Lord is with him."***

[1 Samuel 16:18]

David had all the qualifications and the Lord was also with him as the bible describes it in the above scripture. My Dear reader, having all the qualities without Jesus will lead you to nowhere. How far you can go in this world as a leader is determined by how deep you are rooted in Christ Jesus. Deep root in Christ: higher height on the earth. It came to pass that David ministered to Saul, the King of Israel to have his deliverance. May your service to mankind bring deliverance to people.

*"And so it was, whenever the spirits from God was upon Saul that David would take a harp and play it with his hand. Then Saul would become refreshed and well, and distressing spirit would depart from him."*

*[1 Samuel 16:23]*

Though David did well to King Saul, he had a severe problem with King Saul because of who David could become. Satan is against you because of what God wants you to become. A thorny type of atmosphere was created around him. Saul did not want David to fulfill his destiny.

*"Now Saul Spoke to Jonathan his son and to all his servants that they should kill David..."*

*[1 Samuel 19:1]*

David's life was being monitored by Saul, the King of the land. Sometimes Satan will cause people to monitor your life with the intention of eliminating you from the surface of the earth altogether. All is because of what God wants you to become. King Saul designed different strategies to eliminate David from the earth.

In this kind of atmosphere, thorns are everywhere to choke you. Let's see what happened.

*"Now the distressing spirit from the Lord came upon Saul as he sat in his house with his spear in his hand. And David was playing music with his hand. Then Saul sought to pin David to the wall with his spear,*

***but he slipped away from Saul's presence and he drove the spear into the wall. So David fled and escaped that night"***

[1 Samuel 19:9-10]

When David escaped to his house, Saul still sent his messengers to kill him, but David escaped again. Saul again sent messengers to bring David back so that he could kill him. Don't walk into an unconducive environment no matter what you can get. Please, do not surround yourself with people who are against what you believe and do. If your friends do not believe in what you do, even though you are doing what is right, leave them, they are not your true friends as you may think, but enemies in disguise. In life, it is reasonable to go to where you will be celebrated and not where you will be tolerated.

This kind of atmosphere in these two categories, the physical antagonist and the spiritual antagonist. David's owns was in the physical realm. In fact, he had a direct encounter with Saul, so also was Joseph. The young man Joseph had a direct encounter with his brothers also.

In this situation, you can strategically position yourself in God to handle the situation. As aforesaid, we also have a spiritual antagonist. With spiritual thorns, you face Satan and his messengers who will fight you in discharging your duties as required by God. Satan will see to it that you don't dominate to fulfill God's purpose. Satan will do his best to stop you from dominating.

He will put diseases on you, he will cast weakness on you, he will tempt you to sin against God. He is the accuser of the brethren *[See Revelation 12:10]*. But remember that he has been cast down by Jesus the Saviour. He will send demons to fight and kill you.

Remember that spiritual defeats lead to physical defeats of your destiny.

**"After this, Jesus knowing that all things were accomplished, that the scriptures must be fulfilled, said 'I thirst' and when He had received the sour wine, He said 'it is finished"**

*[John 19:28-30]*

## GOOD ENVIRONMENT

**"But others fell on good ground and yielded a crop; some a hundredfold, some sixty, some thirty."**

*[Matthew 13:8]*

Jesus, after presenting to us the three types of bad environment did not leave it there but added to them a good type of environment. Good ground, atmosphere, or environment is where you are accepted and well accommodated. The air, the water, the texture, and the right nutrient which represents the people, their attitude, their spirit embraces you with love and passion and ready to support you to make it.  It is the type of environment where good and acceptable results are inevitable.  In this type of environment, good fruits are yielded always.

Anytime you find yourself in that type of environment you bear good fruits. The ground is always fertile.  It has the right nutrients to bring forth good fruits.  It has water to nurture the seed.  If you invest in that environment you don't incur losses, but rather a good profit. Good and acceptable fruit-bearing is symbolic of your being in the right environment.

## CREATING YOUR OWN ATMOSPHERE OF PRODUCTIVITY THAT WILL YIELD GOOD FRUIT.

The feeling or mood that you have in a particular place is important because it determines whether you will be productive or not.  It also determines whether you will dominate in life or not.  The feeling you have in a particular environment predicts your success or failure. If that is true, then one must create his or her own atmosphere that will favour him or her.

One must know who he or she is because who you determine where you should be, not the other way round. Every seed needs a particular kind of atmosphere/ environment for it to grow well and bear good fruits. Sugar cane cannot be planted just anywhere for commercial purposes. It grows well in semi-water logged environments, likewise rice.

When planting groundnut you need hard ground with hot temperatures if you want a good yield. If you plant groundnut on waterlogged ground you would not yield any profit, but incur losses. This is because waterlogged environments are not really good for groundnut.

You need to look at the type of person you are, the kind of talent you have, the tempo at which you can assimilate things, your temperaments, etc. When you identify all these qualities in you, then it becomes imperative to know the associates you would mingle with. You need to disassociate from all the wrong people who are there to destroy you.

The Bible commands us to love our neighbours as ourselves *[See Leviticus 19:16],* Jesus also said something about loving our neighbour in the Gospel of Matthew.

***"You have heard that it was said "you shall love your neighbour and hate your enemies." But I say to you, 'love your enemies, bless those who curse you, do good to those who hate you, and pray for those who spitefully use you, who persecute you."***

*[Matthew 5:43-44]*

God told the Israelites in the Old Testament to love each other. Jesus also told us not to love only our loved ones, but our enemies. Loving people is a must as Christians, but befriending people is a matter of choice *[Leviticus*

*19:18].* The fact that you love every man does not mean that you should befriend all. Jesus told us to love our neighbours and not necessarily befriend all our neighbours.

We choose people we want to walk with. Jesus loves everybody, but He chose some selected few to walk with whom He called his disciples. He loved everyone, but He chose His disciples (friends), even among His disciples some were dear to him. *[See John 13:23, John 19:26]*

God has given us the power of choice so we can choose our friends, meaning those people we want to walk with, that does not mean they are the only people you will show love to. The people who can push you forward in life, who would encourage and support you to fulfill your God-given assignment should be your friends. For example, Jonathan assisted David to be successful in fulfilling destiny but Saul wanted to kill him. David did not hate Saul but Jonathan was his friend. If Saul was hated by David he would have killed him when he found him asleep in the cave. *[See 1 Samuel 24:1-11]*

Jesus did not walk with everybody, He had twelve disciples who came to believe in Him and His goals. Jesus went about to call his disciples (friends, Students). He created for Himself the right atmosphere by surrounding Himself with people who accepted His leadership.

*"Now Jesus walking by the Sea of Galilee, saw two brothers, casting a net into the sea; for they were fishermen. "And He (Jesus) said to them; 'follow me ...'[Matthew 4:19].* Follow me means have fellowship with me or befriend me or be my follower. Strategically align yourself with the right people, it will be a blessing to you.

A woman, who knew who Jesus was, strategically associated herself with Him. She was attracted to Jesus by her sacrificial gift. We can learn lessons from her act of sacrifice.

**"Then Mary took a pound of very costly oil of spikenard, anointed the feet of Jesus and wiped His feet with her hair. And the house was filled with the fragrance of the oil."**

*[John 12:3]*

Consider the response of Jesus to the comment passed by Judas Iscariot on what the woman did. "...Why do you trouble the woman, for she has done a good work for me? You have the poor with you always, but me you do not have always. For pouring this fragrant oil on my body, she did it for my burial.

**"Assuredly, I say to you, wherever this gospel is preached in the whole world what this woman has DONE will also be told as a memorial to her."**

*[Mathew 26:1a-13]*

The woman had this pronouncement of blessing from the Lord Jesus. What she did from her heart strategically linked herself to Jesus and she was blessed by the Lord.

*"A man's gift makes room for him and brings him before great men." [Proverbs 18:16].* Your gift will make a room for you

Surround yourself with wise men and you shall be imparted with wisdom.

**"He who walks with wise men shall be wise, but the champion of fools shall be destroyed."**

*[Proverbs 13:20]*

Based on your pursuits; strategically link yourself to those who are already ahead of you in your field of endeavour, get the right information that will help you to get to your destination easily. That is wisdom. In the same manner, a student should do well to connect himself to those ahead of him in his field of study.

## THREE LEVELS OF ASSOCIATION

We have three levels of associations in life; your superiors, your equals as well as your subordinates. Your success in life can be determined by how you relate to these categories of people God has provided. God determines your success in life but the channels through which He blesses you are these classes of people.

How you relate to your superior will determine whether he will promote you or not. How you relate to your equals will determine whether they should come close to you or run away from you. We always share ideas with our equals, since there are some issues we cannot discuss with either our superiors or subordinates. Know how to relate to them in order to attract them.

Finally, how you manage your subordinates is much more essential. If you maltreat them, they will run away from you. They are there to give you certain vital information for your work. If you handle them well they will reveal the secrets of those who are against you. They are very fast in receiving information about their leaders.

## AN ATMOSPHERE OF LOVE

Everyone who wants to dominate in the Kingdom of Jesus Christ should learn to create an atmosphere of love around him or her. People won't love you except you love them first. Love is an attitude we should admonish and develop. Though some people will still hate you even though you show them some kind of love, as long as we have the Holy Spirit as children of God, we can love anyone including our enemies because love is the product of the Holy Spirit who dwells in us. The only way we can win the love of people is to love them. For God to win the people of the world, He first loved them. *"For God so loved the world..." [See John 3: 16]* Human beings create an atmosphere of love when we exhibit love for others.

## AN ATMOSPHERE OF RESPECT

Commanding respect in the society you live is very significant. It puts you on the top and thereby causes you to dominate. Respect comes as a result of the way you act and react. One's attitude towards people determines one's altitude in society. Altitude is the height above sea level. Above sea level means you are at the highest level of respect. Respect at sea level is the normal type of respect. Here, people may not respect you because you command respect.

It may be that you are older than them so they give some kind of respect based on your age. The respect above sea level is exhibited towards a person who commands it, not necessarily because of his age or status in the society, but his character. Here you may be very young but your attitude - that is; your actions and reactions - command that respect. People at the sea level kind of respect sometimes demand respect from the society based on their age, etc.

Lastly, respect below sea level is when you have lost your respect in society. Children may insult you. The whole society sees you as a disgrace. You command respect when you behave well and respect people no matter their age difference, status, educational background, etc.

## PRINCIPLES OF ATTRACTIVE ATMOSPHERE

I would like to give you seven vitamins (principles) that will create for you a very attractive atmosphere.

## PRINCIPLE NUMBER (1)

**Pay attention to people:** Paying attention to people is very important in creating a very attractive atmosphere. People naturally develop love for those who pay attention to them.

## PRINCIPLE NUMBER (2)

**Be presentable:** Here the way you present yourself to people will let them admire you. Dress smartly, smile at people, and be smart in your dealings with them. Listen to them when they talk to you. Answer their questions.

## PRINCIPLE NUMBER (3)

**Caring for People:** Taking care of people, means being passionate. Love generates passion. If someone is in need and you have the means, assist that person.

## PRINCIPLE NUMBER (4)

**Remember Everybody's Name:** Names are for identification. The sweetest sound in everyone's ear is his or her name. Everybody is highly sensitive to his or her name. That is why when a particular name is mentioned in public and you bear that name, you turn to look around to see whether you are the one being called.

## PRINCIPLE NUMBER (5)

**Walk slowly into the crowd:** In any gathering, if you are called to deliver a speech, walk majestically and slowly to the front. The way you walk in public will cause either negative or positive attractions.

## PRINCIPLE NUMBER SIX (6)

**Be generous:** People who are generous generate attraction. Action speaks louder than words. Give to the needy and support the handicapped. Remember, sympathy is always better than apathy.

## PRINCIPLE NUMBER SEVEN (7)

**Enjoy Life:** Life is meant to be enjoyed but not to be endured. The way you see life and how you approach it is very vital. Human beings naturally love to enjoy themselves so if you are a joyous person, people will like to associate themselves with you. Remember celebration attracts, but mourning repels. If you enjoy the gift of life people will be attracted to you.

People are repelled by those who always see the negative side of life. Do not see life as a burden, see it as a gift from God. Always thank God for the gift of life and enjoy its fullness. Excitement generates good health and good health generates longevity. Enjoy the gift of life to the glory of God and you will live long.

These seven vitamins of success will put you on top in life as you implement them. Try to create such an attractive atmosphere for yourself, people will love to work with you to fulfill your fortune.

What is behind you is infinite power, before you are earnest possibilities and around you are boundless opportunities, why then should you fail?

## Power Quote

- The potency of the seeds may be the same, but the different environments under which they grow will determine their outcome.
- The atmosphere you permit determines the attitude you convey.
- The secret behind receiving lies in giving, but whom you give to matters.
- Feeling and action are one, they cannot be separated.
- For thus says the Lord to the men of Judah and Jerusalem: break up your fallow ground and do not sow among thorns. *[Jeremiah 4:3]*

# CHAPTER 7

# UPON YOUR CONFESSION

*"Death and life are in the power of the tongue, and those who have it will eat its fruits"*

[Proverbs 18:21]

In life, you will either dominate or be dominated by your own confession. What proceeds out of your mouth will either kill you or prolong your days. In the land of the living, you will either dominate or be dominated by what you say. I have seen a lot of people who have been imprisoned for their own confessions.

### The Creative Nature of Words

Words are very creative. Words can create good as well as bad things. You are the right person to determine what it creates.

*"In the beginning was the Word..." [John 1:1]* The word has been there since time

immemorial.  In the beginning, was not just a word, but was the word. That means the word has no beginning. The Word was there before the heavens and earth were created. When God was creating heavens and earth, He spoke the word, and His spoken words came reality. Remember, God spoke the word and not a word. The word is different from any other word or some words. Though words are intangible, they have the capacity to be tangible. In fact, the words you speak, if it is in agreement with the word of God, have the potency to come to pass.

**"And the Word became flesh, and dwelt among us, and we beheld His glory..."**

*[John 1:14]*

The word that one speaks can become flesh.  That means it can become tangible or real if your confession agrees with God's word. God's power will bring it to pass in your life. What about words that are not in line with God's word? If what you speak is not in line with the word of God, it will automatically be in favour with the word of satan.

Any word that does not agree with the word of God will not favor you, and if it does not favor you, Satan will also see to it that it comes to pass in your life. That means what everyone says will have either a positive or negative effect on him or her.

Until you believe the word of God and confess it, you will never be saved.

***"For with the heart one believes to righteousness and with the mouth confession is made to salvation"***
*[Romans 10:10]*

What you believe is what you confess and what you confess leads you to salvation or condemnation.

Faith confession is an outward expression of an inward belief, that is to say, that if you confess that you will not prosper you already believe that you will not prosper in your heart. God knows what is in your heart, but He wants you to express it to the world to show that you believe in Him before you can be saved.  God is the God of principles and He will never break His principles.

***"God is not a man, that He should lie. nor a son of man that He should repent. Has He said, and will not do it? Or has He spoken and will not make it good?"***
*[Numbers 23:79]*

Satan does not know what is in your heart and mind unless you voice it out. Satan is not omniscient, only God is. Satan only uses what comes out of your mouth to work against you. So if you are the type that confesses the negatives, "l cannot make it", "it is impossible for me to prosper, "who am I to pass this exam?", "I was born poor and will die destitute", etc., satan will have the permission based on what you say and use your own words to entangle you because he gets to know what you believe based on your own confessions.

Satanic agents are all over the world and their assignment is to make sure that you fail, fall, and fade out if you permit them. The devil doesn't want your true colour to show forth. He knows that your true colour portrays the glory of the True God. Satan is the antichrist, which means he is against Jesus Christ our savior. When you are becoming like Christ by exhibiting God's glory through the obedience of the word of God, he becomes very angry. That is why Satan is against the called-out ones.

## THE HISTORY OF CREATION

The heavens and earth were created by the word of GOD. What God wanted was what He spoke out. If God had kept quiet the world (earth) and the beautiful things therein wouldn't have come into existence. *[See Genesis 1:1]* I encourage you to speak out what you want Jesus to do for you. Let us consider critically these scriptures:

THEN GOD SAID, *"Let there be light"*, and there was light. THEN GOD SAID, *"Let there be a firmament in the midst of the waters, and let it divide the waters from the waters"*.

THEN GOD SAID, *"Let *the waters under the heavens*

*be gathered together into one place and let dry land appear"* and it Was so THEN GOD SAID, *"Let the earth bring forth grass, the herb that yields seed, the fruit tree that yields fruit according to its kind, whose seed is in itself, on the earth,* and it was so THEN GOD SAID, *"Let there be light in the firmament of the heavens to divide the day from the night: and let them be for signs seasons and for days and years: and let them be for lights in the firmament of heavens to give light on the earth"* and it was so.

THEN GOD SAID, *"Let the waters abound with an abundance of living creature, and let birds fly above the earth across the face of the firmament of the Heavens."* THEN GOD SAID, *"Let the earth bring forth the living creatures according to its kind: cattle and creeping things and beast of the earth each according to its kind"*, and it was so.

THEN GOD SAID, *"Let us make man in our image according to our likeness. Let them have dominion over the fish of the sea, over the birds of the air, and over every creeping thing that creeps in the earth,"* So God created man in His own image: in the image of God He created him, male and female He created them.

AND GOD SAID; *see I have given you every herb that yields seed which is on the face of the earth and every tree whose fruit yields seed: to you shall be for food.*

***Then God saw everything that he had made and indeed
it was very good.***

*[Genesis 1:3-37]*

Looking at the above scriptures, you could see that the
heavens, the earth, and their natural laws came into
existence by the pronouncement of the word of God.

Light came into reality through the spoken words of
God. God saw everything that he had made, and it was
good. If we want to see what we want, we have to utter
them boldly. For example, if we need light in our life, we
have to order it to appear. Light illuminates so also the
word of God illuminates us in the affairs of this world.
The demarcations of the waters from the land came as a
result of what God spoke. Plants came into existence by
the commandment of God. Times and seasons came into
reality when God spoke. Living creatures in the heavens,
the earth, and in the sea came into manifestation by the
spoken word of God.

The idea of creating man was voiced out by God before
man was created, and so man is a product of God's word.
*[See Genesis 1:26a, John.1:3]*

## WHERE IS GOD RESIDING?

As a Christian, God is residing in you in the form of His
word.

## YOU ARE THE PRODUCT OF YOUR WORD

In fact, human beings are the product of the word of God. Your state in life is also the product of your own words and actions and the word that governs you.

If you want to assess the spirit of a man, engage him in a conversation for some time. At the end of the conversation based on his words, you will know who that person is. You are what you say and do. That is why when a president is invited to an occasion and he is hard-pressed, he delegates one of his ministers to attend that occasion in his stead. The minister reads the president's message to the gathering. The words of the message are the words of the president and not the minister. People will assess the president by the word read on his behalf and if there is any question or demand, it will be forwarded to the president through a report by the minister. People will know that you are dominating in society by your own words. Who you are today is the result of what you spoke and did some years ago.

Do not curse yourself by your own mouth, speak good things into your life. Be convinced and say what God says you are in faith. Consider what you speak to yourself, family, friends, etc., very well because it can lead you or those you speak to into victory or defeat.

Dear friend, do not curse yourself with your mouth; rather bless your life with the word of God. Bless your children with the word of God. Bless your nation with





*"On that day you will know that I am in my father and you in me and I in you."*

*[John 14:20]*

God the Son (Jesus) dwells in you and God the Holy Spirit dwells in you. "If you abide in Me, and My words abide in you, you will ask what you desire and it shall be done for you" (John 15:7).

Jesus resides in you in the form of His word, because He is the word of God.

### *"...And the Word was God"*

*[John 1:1]*

If you have the word of God in you which was used to change the atmosphere when the earth was without form and was void, and darkness was upon the face of the deep, then the same word of God which is in you as a Christian can be used to change the atmosphere if the atmosphere does not favour you. In the beginning, when God saw that the earth He had created was without form, and void and darkness were on the face of the deep, He did not like it. This made the Almighty God speak his desires into being.

Keep on confessing the Word of God in faith as you act upon it and your situation will change to your advantage. Confession of the Word of God in faith is a form of prayer. You may not have anything physically, but as long as you have the Word of God you have everything. Amen.

The atmospheric world was created out of the Word of God. Create a suitable atmosphere for yourself by the usage of the Word of God. The words of God that you speak will one day become flesh *[See John 1:14]*. You may be poor, yet speak the word of God that says, *"...I am rich." [1 Corinthians. 4:8]* You may be weak, yet say as it is written, *"Let the weak say, I am strong" [Joel 3: 10b]*, you may need money make the faith confession that all my need shall be supplied. *[See Philippians 14:19]* Be filled with the Word of God. Confess it in faith continually and you shall see it in reality at the fullness of time. If you believe the Word of God as you confess it you shall have whatever you say in line with the will of God. The Word of God is the principle of God and therefore, it cannot be broken.

**"And the scriptures (My Word) cannot be broken."**

*[John 10:35]*

## WORDS ARE SPIRIT AND LIFE
*It is the spirit who gives life, the flesh profit nothing. The words that I speak to you are spirit, and they are life.*

*[John 6:63]*

Human beings are tripartite in nature. We are spirit, soul, and body. According to theBible; it is the spirit that is





in man that gives him or her life. Your body is alw inactive without your spirit. That is why when the s] of man departs from a person, the body becomes inac and therefore considered dead.

The body becomes useless as soon as the spirit of r is departed. Jesus knowing this said, *"The words th speak unto you, they are spirit and they are life." [Jo 6:63]* The word of God is a spirit and it brings life dead situations. That is why someone who is downc or even dead can be uplifted by the word of God *[Ezel 37:1-14]*

When you wake up in the morning, you need to prophe to yourself by the word of God. When you do that t spirit of God in you will respond to that word of fai (prophecy) and your spirit that responds to the word God will activate your body for effective discharge your duties ahead of the day.

Keep on speaking life to yourself and your fai confession will come to pass in Jesus' name. For it written,

**"Blessed is she that believed; for there shall be performance of those things which were told her fron the Lord"**

*[Luke 1:45*

the word of God because that is the place God in his own wisdom gave you.

**Power Quote**

- For good or evil, your conversation is your advertisement.
- Anytime you open your mouth you expose your mind to the world.
- For we all stumble in many things. If anyone does not stumble in word; he is a perfect man, who is able to bridle the whole body."
- Do your best to handle your tongue with wisdom. It will lead you to blessings.

*"With our mouth, we bless our God and Father, and with it, we curse men, who have been made in the sameness of God. Out of the same mouth proceed blessing and cursing. My brethren, these ought not to be so."*

*[James 3:9-10]*

CHAPTER **8**

# WHAT AM I HEARING?

For a person to dominate in life, hearing goes a long way to affect whether or not it will be possible. God gave us five senses and one of our senses is that of hearing. The ear is the channel through which we receive verbal information. The ear is a blessing to man. God gave man the power of choice. Man can choose what he or she wants to give attention to, even though sometimes you may not choose to hear something, but it enters into your ears. But let us thank God for giving us the choice to listen. Listening goes beyond hearing. Listening is a deliberate act whiles hearing may not always be deliberate. You may be passing by and may not choose to listen to the tumult going on, but you will hear it.

Listening is giving attention to one particular sound wave. What we listen to is more important in life because it goes a long way to determine whether or not we will dominate as God intended for us.

The definition of the word hearing in the Oxford Learner's dictionary is, *"to be aware of sounds with your ears."* You could see that it is not deliberately done. The same dictionary defines listening as "paying attention to something or somebody you can hear."

Listening develops understanding, but hearing does not. You can hear without learning. If you listen to something, say music, you can get the words and the meaning, but you may not get the very words and the meaning by just hearing the music. In this chapter, the focus will turn to what we give our attention to. That is what we listen to. What we listen to is much more important in our life pursuit. It goes a long way to affect us either positively or negatively. It depends on what we are listening to.

***"So faith comes by hearing and hearing by the word of God"***

*[Romans 10: 17]*

According to God's word, faith comes by hearing the word of God. So also fear comes by hearing and hearing of the beliefs of the world. Do you know that false ideology can be seen as truth if one listens to it again and again? The Bible talks about how faith is developed. It comes by hearing and by hearing the word of God. The phrase "hearing and by hearing" means 'listening to'. It is giving attention to a particular sound wave. You do it again and again. The more you continue to listen to the word of God, the more your faith grows. If you look at the circumstances and the atmosphere of the world: how evil is becoming rampant, how accidents are becoming the order of the day, how the numbers of murders are increasing, how diseases abound, etc., you will develop fear.

I will urge you to give your attention to the word of God, meditating over it in order for your faith to grow strong. It is only the spirit of faith that can overcome the spirit of fear. Anytime faith is enthroned in one's life, fear is dethroned.

There is a story in the Bible that gives a vivid picture with a clear understanding of the effect of what we listen to.  Let us consider the scripture below.

*"So Moses sent them out to spy the land of Canaan and said to them 'Go up this way into the south and go up to the mountains and see what the land is like: whether the people who dwell in it are weak or strong, few or many: whether  the land they dwell in is good or bad; whether the cities they inhabit are like camps or strongholds;*

*Whether the land is rich or poor; and whether  there are forests there or not. Be of good courage and bring back some of the fruits of the land.  Now the time was the season of the first ripe grapes.  So they went up and spied out the land from the wilderness of Zin as far as Rehob  they went up through the south and came to Hebron; Ahiman, Sheshai and Talmai. The descendants of Anak were there. (Now Hebron was built seven years before Zoan in Eggpt) Then they came to the valley of Eshcol and there cut down a branch with one cluster of grapes; they carried it between two men on a pole. They also brought some of the pomegranates and figs. The place was called the valley of Eshcol because of the cluster which the men of Israel cut down there. And they returned from spying the land after forty days. So they departed and came back to Moses and Aaron and all the congregation of the children of Israel in the wilderness of Paran and Kadesh,  they brought back word to them and to all the congregation and showed them the fruit of the land.*

*Then they told him and said; "We went to the land where you sent us.  It truly flows with milk and honey, and this is the fruit. Nevertheless the people who dwell in the land are strong: the cities are fortified and very large; moreover we saw the descendants of Anak there. The Amalekites dwell in the land of the south; the Hittites, the Jebusites and the Amoites dwell in the mountains; and the Canaanites dwell by the sea and along the banks of the Jordan." Then Caleb quieted the people before Moses and said, 'Let us go up at once and take possession; for we are well able to overcome it'.*

*BUT the men who had gone with him said, 'We are not able to go up against the people for they are stronger than we." Then they gave the people of Israel a bad report of the land which they have spied out, saying "The land through which we have gone as spies is the land that devours its inhabitant, and all the people who we saw in it are men of great stature. There we saw the giants (The descendants of Anak came from the giants) and we were like grasshoppers in our own sight and so we were in their sight" Then the entire congregation lifted up their voice and cried and the people wept that night.*

*[Numbers 13:11-33 :14-7]*

Do not walk with faithless people because they always see the negative part of life instead of the positive.

Before Moses sent out the twelve spies to go and spy on the land of Canaan, the children of Israel engaged in several battles and won.  Before they were released by Pharaoh, God used Moses to perform mighty miracles in Egypt. On their way to Canaan, God used Moses to divide the Red Sea. *[See Exodus 14:21- 22]*. In the wilderness, God provided them with Manna when they needed food. (Exodus 16).  Bitter water was turned sweet when there was a scarcity of water. *[See Exodus 15:22-27]* Water came from rocks when they were in need of it *[See Exodus 17:1-17]*.  They defeated the Amalekites in battle. *[See Exodus 17:8]*

God did a lot of miracles in the sight of the Israelites, yet when they gave attention to the faithless report, they exhibited fear instead of faith in God.  They could not enter the promised land to experience the rest God promised them because of unbelief. *[See Hebrew3:19]*

Moses sent twelve spies to spy on the land, but only two of them could bring a good report. These two were able to enter the promised land because they trusted the Almighty God that He is able by making a faithful statement. The majority of the spies came back with a negative report, and those who believed their confession did not enter into the promised land with Joshua and Caleb.

Faithless people don't have a good message for you no matter their number. That means if the majority do not trust God, they will not win the battle. Caleb tried to stir up the congregation's faith but the ten did not do that. In verse 31 of Number 13, the ten said to the whole congregation that they would not be able to defeat the inhabitants of the land because they are stronger than them. These ten had not fought the inhabitants of the land, but they claimed to be weaker people as compared to the inhabitants of the land of Canaan.

Never admit failure until you have made your last attempt and never make your last attempt until you succeed.

The Bible says that the ten gave the children of Israel a bad report of the land which they had spied. They told the people that they were too weak to fight the inhabitants of the land. This made the whole congregation afraid of going to possess the land. The Bible says, that night, 'the entire congregation lifted up their voice and cried.' They all wept that night. *[See Numbers 14:1]*

In the end, the whole congregation of Israel could not enter the promised land which the LORD had promised, because of what they listened to. They gave their attention to the evil report of the ten spies instead of the good report of the two spies who were Joshua and Caleb.

## WHAT YOU LISTEN TO AFFECTS YOU

What you give your attention to affects your emotions and changes your mood or feelings. In the above scripture, two reports were submitted to the Israelites, but they chose to listen to the ten and rejected the two. They heard what Joshua and Caleb said, but did not give their attention to it. If you give the devil attention, he will give you directions.

I have seen a man who was celebrating his birthday party in a foreign land. This man became very sad after receiving an unpleasant phone call that his mother had been knocked down by a vehicle and had died. His beautiful countenance instantly changed as he heard the report. I have also seen a gentleman who faced difficulties in life, but all of a sudden became happy after he had been appointed the manager of a firm.

Beloved, we should be very circumspective with what we listen to or give rapt attention to. If you give your attention to people who tell you that you can't make it, you are likely to fail, even though you might be doing the right thing. Their words are likely to affect your emotions negatively and discourage you from doing what you are doing.  The way people see you is different from the way God sees you.

 The way God sees you can be seen through the lenses of the Bible i.e., the written word of God. It is important to give your attention to the Word of God and your world (system) will change for the better.

Listen to the voice behind the written Word showing you the way not the noise of the world confusing you. *[See Isaiah 30:21]*

**"Give ear, Oh my people, to my law; Incline your ears to the words of my mouth'.**

*[Psalm78:7]*

**"The Word of God is wisdom listen to it. "My son, if you receive my words, and treasure my commands within you so that you incline your ears to wisdom and your  heart to understanding. "**

*[Proverbs 2:1-2]*

**"My son, give your attention to my words: incline your ears to my sayings"**

*[Proverbs 4:20]*

**"According to the Word of God, what you hear can corrupt or deform you. "Do not be deceived, evil communication corrupts good manners"**

*[1 Corinthians 15:33]*

What we listen to is of great importance such that getting to the last chapters of the book of Revelations, God told us to listen to what the Spirit says to us.

*"He who has an ear let him hear what the Spirit says to the churches." [Revelations 2:7]*
*"He who has an ear let him hear what the Spirit says to the churches." [Revelations 2:11]*
*"He who has an ear let him hear what the Spirit says to the churches." [Revelations 2:7]*
*"He who has an ear let him hear what the Spirit says to the churches." [Revelations 2:7]*
*"He who has an ear let him hear what the Spirit says to the churches." [Revelations 2:2-9]*
*"He who has an ear let him hear what the Spirit says to the churches." [Revelations 3:6]*
*"He who has an ear let him hear what the Spirit says to the churches." [Revelations 3:7-3]*
*"He who has an ear let him hear what the Spirit says to the churches." [Revelations 3:22]*
*"If anyone has an ear let him hear." [Revelation 7:3-9]*

Dear reader, allow the Word of God and the spirit of God to influence you. Give God your attention and He will give you direction.

## Power Quotes

- Your philosophies in life come as a result of the information you have accumulated.

# CHAPTER 9

# DOMINION IS YOUR BIRTHRIGHT

*"And God said; let us make man in our image, after our likeness: and let them have dominion over..."*

*[Genesis 1:26]*

Taking total dominion over other creatures of God and overcoming the system of the world is your birthright as a Christian. In the above scripture, we see God voicing out His intention for which man is to be created. "Let them have dominion," says God. The creator created you so that you can take dominion over his creatures. You were created to dominate so you can't afford to be dominated by situations, circumstances, and demons as a believer. Actually, man is destined by God to dominate on earth.

To dominate is to control and have total influence over something. In fact, it is when we take dominion that we discharge our responsibilities as stewards of God. Jehovah God purposely destined man to occupy the earth and subdue it. God who is in heaven is the ruler of the heavens and the earth and all therein. The Bible says that God's throne is the heavens and the earth His footstool.

*"Thus says the Lord, The heaven is my throne and earth is my footstool" (Isaiah 66:1a) God's glory fills the heavens. "God's glory fills the heavens."*

*[7 kings 8:11]*

The way by which God's glory manifest on the earth is when God's commandments (spoken words) come to pass.

*"Then God said, 'let us make man in our image, according to our likeness; let them have dominion over the fish of the sea, over the birds of the air, over the cattle, over all the earth and over every creeping thing that creeps on the earth"*

*[Genesis 1:26]*

Taking total dominion over other creatures of God is a command that God gave to man. God's statement in the above scripture wasn't a suggestion. A suggestion is an optional statement, but a commandment is obligatory. Taking total dominion is a must and therefore ought to be seen in our lives. God takes pleasure in us when we obey His commandments. God's word must surely come to pass.

*"So shall my word be that goes forth out of my mouth; it shall not return to me void, but it shall accomplish what I please, and it shall prosper in the things for which I sent it."*

*[Isaiah 55:11]*

God Himself sees to it that what proceeds out of His mouth comes to pass. What pleases God is what comes out of His mouth. *[See Numbers 23:79]*

Because God's word must come to pass, He gives us what it takes to fulfill it. God knowing that man is fallible because of sin, provided the way for him to overcome any form of temptation that may come his or her way.

*"No temptation has overtaken you except what is common to man; but God is faithful who will not allow you to be tempted beyond what you are able, but with the temptation will also make a way of escape that you may be able to bear it."*

*[1 Corinthians 10:13]*

It is God who gives us the power to fulfill our destiny. The knowledge of God the father, son, and Holy Spirit gives us everything we need for life and godliness.

*"As his divine power has given to us all things that pertain to life and godliness through him who called us by glory and virtue."*

*[2 Peter 1:3]*

With these, man can dominate the earth by obeying every word that comes out of the mouth of God. Destiny is what must surely come to pass. Destiny or birthright is always unalterable or immutable. If we try to avoid what God has ordained for us we mess up with our lives.

Dear friend, if you are ready to fulfill God's will then He will grant you the grace and power to fulfill it. What you have to do to fulfill God's intent for your life is to discover it by desiring it, because it is only when you desire that you discover. When you discover what your destiny is, God will grant you the grace to fulfill it. King David considered the position and destiny of man and said;

What is man that you are mindful of him? For you hope made him o little lower than angels and you have crowned him with glory and honour. You have made him to have dominion over the works of your hand; you ' have put all things under his feet, All the sheep and oxen and even the beast of the field. The birds of the air and the fish of the sea, that passes through the path of the sea. *[See Psalm 8:4-8]*

**IMITATORS OF CHRIST**

The word imitate is a verb. One definition of the word imitate is *"to copy the behaviour of somebody or something (Take or follow as an example)"*

Christians have only one perfect role model. He is in the person of Jesus Christ. Jesus is the second in command of the Godhead. Jesus Christ is God but incarnated as man. Jesus Christ exhibited the very character of God when He was on earth as a perfect man. We as Christ's followers are to imitate his life. If we imitate Him as his followers we will portray the very character of God.

Imitating nobody, but Jesus Christ is perfect living in God to man. You can only imitate Jesus Christ by accepting him as your Lord and saviour and obeying the word of God. Obeying the word of God leads to perfection and breeds dominion. In fact, you become perfect as you obey his word because his word is perfect.

**"Therefore you shall be perfect, just as your father in heaven is perfect."**

[Matthew 5 :48]

## THE PURPOSE

The subject matter here is what leads to total dominion. Perfection is the only way to total dominion. Perfection in the sight of God is doing the will of God. This comes as a result of obedience to the word of God. The will of God brings glory to God. God created us purposely to exhibit his glory on earth. So man in a good relationship with his creator is the glory of God on earth. *"Everyone who is called by My name whom I have created for My glory; I have formed him, yes I have made him."* [Isaiah 43:7]

When man sinned, He fell short of the glory of God. *[See Romans 3: 23]* Man who has been created to exhibit the glory of God came short of the glory of God. When the glory departed, man became subject to shame. Sickness took charge of our lives and the end of it was death.

The purpose of Jesus Christ's coming was to restore us into God's glory. The only way by which Christ could do that was to defeat the power of sin and to destroy the works of the devil.

**"He who sins is of the devil, for the devil has sinned from the beginning. For this purpose the son of man was manifested, that he might destroy the works of the devil"**

*[7 John 3:8]*

Remember that Jesus Christ did not come to kill the devil but to destroy his works which led to shame and death.

**RESTORATION OF DOMINION**
The purpose was to restore man back to God's glory and dominion and was to destroy the power of sin which leads to death. How did Jesus Christ destroy the works of Satan and how can we do that?

Jesus Christ overcame death by living in holiness (that is obeying God's word); so the only way we can overcome death is by living in Christ. *[See Acts 17:27]* Jesus Christ dominated over unclean spirits by living in righteousness. Righteousness means right standing with God. Jesus said;

**"The prince of this world is coming but he has nothing in me."**

*[John 14:3a]*

This was because Jesus stood right with God. He positioned himself in the word of God so therefore the devil could not cause him harm. We ought to stand for righteousness and we will dominate Satan.

Again, Jesus Christ calmed the storm by exercising faith in God the Father. *[See Mark 4:39]* We can dominate the storms of life by exhibiting faith in God through His word.  Jesus Christ overcame confusion by preaching the Gospel which is love, peace, and righteousness. *[See Luke4:43]* Jesus Christ overcame the world (the system of governance) by obeying the Word of God and doing what God does. *[See John 16:33]*

Jesus Christ healed the sick by discharging his authority in God by faith. We are to do the same because we have been given the same authority from above. *[See Matthew 28:19, Luke 10:19]* Believers of Jesus Christ have been given the grace to live, do and teach what Jesus taught. *[See Mark 16:15, Acts 1:1]*

Those who live in Christ and do and teach what Jesus did and taught, will certainly overcome evil situations and dominate the world. *[See Actsl:1, John 16:33]* Our lifestyle as believers should be like that of Jesus Christ. He has given us the requisite power to tread upon snakes and scorpions and nothing will by any means hurt us. *[See Luke 10:19]* When we address situations by the word of God by faith in Jesus' name, it will give way.

**"Thanks be to God who gives us victory through Christ Jesus."**

*[1 Corinthians 15:57]*

As imitators of Jesus Christ, we have been called upon to destroy the works of satan in order to live in dominion and portray God's glory on earth. Anything that exalts itself against the knowledge of God is of the Devil (2 Corinthians 10:5). Ruling over situations and circumstances of the world is in line with the will of God. Ruling over sin, sickness, and satanic agenda is destroying the works of the devil.The preaching of God's love, peace, and righteousness is in agreement with God's word. If you stand against anything that does not bring glory to God and you support that which brings glory to God, you are fulfilling destiny. Standing against heretic teaching is the work of God. Feeding the hungry is God's work' *[See Romans l2:2a)*. Restoring love and unity through the medium of God's word is acceptable by Christ.

Jesus dominated the world when He Conquered sin and sickness. As a Christian, you are the ambassador of

Christ and therefore you are in the position to dominate as Christ did. Jesus assures us that we will do greater things if we believe in him.

*"Most assuredly, I say to You, he who believes in Me, the works I do he will do also; and greater works than these will he do' because I go to my father."*

[John14:12]

Remember that the bible says,
*"You are of God little children and have overcome them because He who is in you is greater than he who is in the world."*

[1 John 4:4]

Perfectly imitating Jesus Christ is perfectly dominating the world. The way He lived His life on earth is the way Jehovah wants us to live our lives as Christians on the earth. How Jesus Christ dominated Satan, sin, sickness, and shame is the same way God expects from us on earth.

To be frank with you my dear, dominion is your birthright. You are born again to dominate as a Christian so you cannot afford to be dominated. Jesus has shown us the way of God and so let us walk through it.

I pray. for you and with you that you will walk in the counsel of the Almighty God. If you have not accepted the Lord Jesus Christ as your Lord and personal saviour, I urge you in Jesus' name to do so now otherwise your life is doomed, but if you have welcomed Christ into your life then continue to dominate in His name.

> **Power Quote**
>
> - You are born a child of destiny so you cannot afford to die destitute.
> - You are not born of the Spirit of God to suffer again but to dominate.

# CHAPTER 10

# PRAYERS POSITION YOU WELL

Prayer is very essential in our quest for total dominion. What is prayer? Prayer is communication between God and man in the acceptable language - the will/word of God, by the help (conviction) of the Holy Spirit in the name of Jesus Christ. It can simply be defined as the means by which humanity seeks the help of divinity. God is the creator of the heavens and earth. *[See Genesis 1:1]* All power belongs to God. All power whether in heavens, earth, beneath the earth, and even in the sea belongs to Jehovah. God who owns all the powers gave man the delegated authority to take dominion over the earth.

The grace to dominate comes from God. The only means by which man receives such grace to discharge his responsibilities is through prayer in the name of Jesus Christ based on the word of God. It is the Holy Spirit who empowers us to dominate the earth. *[See 2 Peter 1:3-5]* The fact that God intended us to have dominion over His other creatures does not mean that we can dominate without His grace which helps us to obey His commandments. Praying to God always for help is a symbol that you depend on Him. God did not intend for us to depend on our own strength. For it is written,

***"Lean (depend) not on your own understandings, in all your ways acknowledge Him and He shall direct your path."***

*[Proverbs 3:5-6]*

If one needs power, honour, and riches, one needs to ask from God. *[See Proverbs 8:18]* If one needs wisdom one needs to ask from God. *[See James 1:5]* God has made it in such a way that we need to depend on Him totally before we can fulfill His command-taking dominion over the earth.

## PRAYER IS FELLOWSHIP

Prayer as aforesaid is communication between man and his Creator. In prayer, we talk to God and He also talks to us. The more we pray (communicate with God) the more we know His will. The more we know God's will and do it, the more we receive from Him. The more we receive from God the more we do exploit.

***"The people who know their God will be strong and do great exploits"***

*[Daniel 11 : 32]*

But you do not believe because you are not of my sheep as I said to you. *"My sheep hear my voice" [John 70:26-27].* You cannot hear the voice (the Rhema) of God behind the written word of God until you know Him. Communication solidifies relationships.

Lack of communication leads to a lack of knowledge which in turn results in a lack of strength. If you are not strong, you can easily be destroyed, and when you are destroyed you perish.

**"My people are destroyed for lack of knowledge"**
*[Hosea 4:8]*

When we engage in prayers and study the Word, God reveals Himself to us. Moses in the book of Exodus saw God and the children of Israel on top of Mount Sinai.

They sanctified themselves three days in order to meet Jehovah God. They went to the top of the mountains to pray. The Bible says as they prayed, God revealed Himself to them. *[See Exodus 24:9-11]*

Moses had a personal encounter with God through prayers. Moses who was leading the Israelites, one day had an encounter with God when God told him to meet Him in prayer.

Then the Lord said to Moses,

*"Come up to me on the mountain and be there and I will give you tablets of stones and the law and commandments which I have written so you may teach them."*

[Exodus 24:12]

In those days people went to the mountain top to pray to God. Anytime one wanted to pray, he isolated himself from the people to go to the mountain top to pray. Prayer is worship according to God's word so they needed concentration. When one worships God, one needs concentration.

*"Our fathers worshiped on this mountain and you Jesus say that in Jerusalem is the place where we ought to worship."*

[John 4:20]

The glory of God is in His presence. Anytime you engage yourself in communication with God through worship, you saturate yourself with the glory of God to dominate the earth.

*"Then Moses went up to the mountains and a cloud covered the mountain, now, the glory of the Lord rested on Mount Sinai."*

[Exodus 24:75-16]

Where God is, His glory abounds. The glory of God is like a consuming fire. It consumes that which is evil and will lead you into destruction in and around you. That is why the word says, "where the spirit (presence) of God is there is liberty." *[See 2 Corinthians 3:17]* The glory of the Lord refines that which is good in you to make it better for domination.

Also, the glory of the Lord protects you from external hostilities. When people with diabolic mind, spirit, and body come to fight you, they cannot defeat you.

Furthermore, God's glory beautifies you to dominate.

Dear folks taking total dominion also lie in your fellowship with God:

## PRAYER IS WORSHIP
*"Our fathers worshiped on this mountain and you Jews say that in Jerusalem is the place where we ought to worship."*

*[John 4:20]*

When we pray, we worship God.  Worship is part of prayer. The one you pray to and worship becomes the one you submit to. You believe in God that He is able to do what you ask. This helps you to acknowledge Him in all your ways.

***"In all your ways acknowledge Him; and He will direct your path."***

*[Proverbs 3:6]*

Acknowledging God in all your ways is humility. It also portrays God's sovereignty over your life. Sovereignty in the biblical context means God exercises His power over all His creation. When we worship God in prayer, we are acknowledging His supremacy. We acknowledge God for who he is and how He is, etc. We glorify God in His presence with our voices and hearts. In fact, when we worship God, our beauty is portrayed in God's presence. God desires our beauty, but it is only exposed when we worship Him *[See Psalm 45:11]*

Worshiping God in prayer connects us to God's glory, power, riches, wisdom, honour, strength, and blessing which in turn lead us to total dominion over the world.

**SEVEN SEALED BLESSINGS FOR DOMINANCE**
These are the seven sealed blessings for those who worship God. Seven is a number of content. God gives us perfect and complete blessings in order for us to have total dominion. All Christians who worship God in spirit and in truth are entitled to these sealed blessings which were unfolded by Jesus Christ in His glory.

***"You are worthy to take the scroll and open its seals. For you were slain and have redeemed us to God by Your blood out of every tribe and tongue and people***

*and nation. And have made us kings and priests to our God, and we shall reign on earth." 'Worthy is the lamb who was slain to receive pouter and riches and wisdom and strength and honor and glory and blessing!' and every creature which is in heaven and on earth and under the earth and such as in the sea and all that 'is in them, I heard saying: "Blessing and honor and glory and power are to Him who sits on the throne and to the Lamb forever."*

*[Revelations 5:9-10, 12-13]*

Because Jesus gave God the highest level of worship by obeying God's commandments even unto death, He was empowered and worthy to take and open its seals. *[See Rev 5:9; Acts 4:27-28]*

Taking total dominion lies in your level of humility to worship and reverence God. The more you humble yourself to worship and reverence God, the greater your influence and dominion on earth.

## THE OIL FOR INFLUENCE

The oil for influence is part of what we receive from God when we engage in the act of prayer, worship, and fellowship. God anoints our heads with the Holy Ghost and with the power to do exploits. When someone is anointed, he or she receives the grace and power to function well in his or her area of call. When you are anointed, you receive the very spirit of God to fulfill your destiny on earth. *[See Luke 4:18, Acts 10:38]*

Before Saul became king over the children of Israel, he was anointed, which means he was empowered by God to function as king over the people of God.

*"Then Samuel took a flask of oil and poured it on his head and kissed him and said: 'Is it not because the Lord has anointed you commander over His inheritance?"*

*[1 Samuel 10:1]*

God anointed Saul to rule over His inheritance. He received the anointing from God to have influence over God's inheritance - the children of Israel.

You receive the Spirit of God that will enable you to dominate what God has entrusted to you.

*"Then the Spirit of God came upon him and he prophesied among them."*

*[1 Samuel 10:70]*

Saul who could not prophesy prophesied when he was anointed because the spirit of the Lord God came upon him. Another person who received the grace to rule (dominate) by the influence of the Spirit of God through the channel of the anointing was David. The Bible records that the spirit of the Lord came upon him from that day forward when he was anointed with oil. *[See 1 Samuel 16:13]*

Our Lord Jesus Christ received his earthly anointing at the time of baptism when the Spirit of the Lord came upon him in the form of a dove. *[See Matthew 13:16-17]* He was anointed in order to perform His assignment. He received the anointing to preach the gospel, to heal the brokenhearted, to preach deliverance to the captives, to restore sight to the blind, to liberate the oppressed, and to preach the acceptable year of the Lord's time of deliverance/ salvation. *[See Luke 4: 18-19]*

This is what Doctor Luke said about Jesus Christ in his book.

**"How God anointed Jesus of Nazareth with the holy spirit and with power, who went about doing good and healing all who were oppressed by the devil, for God was with Him."**

*[Acts 10:38]*

Remember that God was with Him. The anointing is what comes upon you to facilitate the fulfillment of your destiny (assignment on earth). When we pray to God, He anoints us to perform His Will. Praying to God is an act of submissiveness. It is a sign that you accept that your ability to do is limited, so He who is limitless should help you.

Throughout the life of Jesus Christ on earth, He prayed all day and all night *[See Luke 6:12]*. Jesus who is all-knowing God did not ignore prayers but rather encouraged his followers to pray all the time.

*"Then He spoke a parable unto them saying that a man should pray and not to lose heart."*

*[Luke 18:1]*

Praying to God always portrays the level of faith you have in Him.  When you depend on God in prayer, He gives you the grace to discharge His own will for your life which leads you to peace on earth. When you pray, you receive strength from God to fulfill your destiny. Jesus prayed while on his way to the cross.

*"Father, if it is your will, remove this cup from me; nevertheless not my  will but yours be done." Then an angel appeared to Him -from Heaven strengthening Him.*

*[Luke 22:42-43]*

Jesus being the Son of God received strength from His Father to fulfill His mission when He prayed. Where will your help come from? Your help comes from God the father. David being a man who pleased God in his generation foresaw this and said in his prayers:

*"May the Lord answer you in the trouble, May the name of the God of Jacob defend you, May He send you help from the sanctuary, and strengthen you out of Zion.*

*[Psalm 20:2]*

Prayer releases the helping hand of God upon you. You receive divine strength in His presence when you engage yourself in prayers. When you pray to God, you are telling God that He is your refuge, strength, and your helper. *[See Psalm 46:1]*

Receiving the strength and help of God is receiving grace and power of God to have influence and fulfill your missions on the earth.

## PRAYER PUTS YOU WHERE YOU BELONG

After God had created man and put him in the Garden of Eden, man did not know sin.

***"Then the Lord God put the man in the Garden of Eden to tend (dress) and keep it."***

*[Genesis 2:15]*

Man discharged his duties in a perfect manner when he was in the state of holiness. Man named all the living creatures in the Garden of Eden. *[See Genesis 2:20]* Whatever man called each living creature became its name. That tells you the level of influence man had on God's creation. All this influence was made possible because of the fact that man was as holy as God his creator. Man dominated everything in the garden. He dressed the Garden of Eden and kept it intact.

In Genesis chapter 3, man sinned against God by disobeying his commandment. He ate of that which God had told him not to eat. The Lord God commanded the man saying,

***"Of every tree in the garden, you may freely eat. But of the tree of the knowledge of good and evil, you may not eat, for in the day that you eat of it, you shall surely die."***

*[Genesis 2:16-17]*

***"So when the woman saw that the tree was good for food that it was pleasant to the eyes and a tree desirable to make one wise, she took of it ate and also gave her husband and he ate."***

*[Genesis 3:6]*

Man lost his position as dominator because sin had taken charge of his life (P. 24). Death which is the reward of sin dominates man. Sickness, fear, poverty, and a host of others, have since dominated man.

Adam and Eve dislocated themselves from where God had located them.

*"... and THERE HE PUT the man whom He had formed"* *[Genesis 2:86]* Adam and his wife hid from the presence of the Lord God.

***"Then the Lord God called out to Adam and said to him, 'where are thou?"***

*[Genesis 3:9]*

The question of where you are has something to do with location and position. They were not in the presence and position of God. They were not taking charge of what God had given to them. They were dislocated from their duty post. Sin took them away from where they belong and so they could not express themselves. They were quarantined in a corner instead of them being in charge of their original place.

## HOLIEST OF HOLIES

The phrase "holiest of holies" represents the very presence of God. God told the children of Israel to consecrate themselves before they could meet Him *[See Exodus 19:9-11]* They met God on His Holy Mountain. *[See Psalm 48:1]*

One goes to the holiest of holies with a prepared heart. Your heart must be renewed and holy. *[See Psalm 51:10-11]* When you have a holy heart you enter into the throne room of grace with all boldness as the book of Hebrews 4:16 says. The throne room of grace is the presence of God. Actually, it was where Adam and Eve were placed they were created before they disobeyed God's words (commands) which caused them to be sacked.

It is only the blood of Jesus that can wash us to enable us to enter into the holiest of holies which is the presence of God, the father. This is revealed to us in the Holy Scriptures;

**"Therefore brethren, having boldness to enter the holiest by the blood of Jesus by a new living way which He consecrated for us through the veil which is his flesh."**

*[Hebrews 10:19-20]*

For your information, Jesus is the holiest of holies. When one comes into Jesus Christ and accepts him as his Lord that person has entered into the holiest of holies that his Father talks about. In Christ Jesus, you qualify to overcome sin, principalities, powers, thrones, dominions, spiritual host of wickedness, etc. You live in the presence of God the father when you are in Christ Jesus. It is through prayer that you communicate with God, through prayers of confession of one's sins that you invite Jesus into your life. Through prayers, your sins are forgiven. It is through prayers one intercedes on behalf of others. *[See Romans 10:9-11]*

After one has repented and prayed for forgiveness, one is put in the state of holiness. Holiness means separation for God's purpose and therefore holiness prepares you for Godly works. Praying to accept Jesus into your life in faith puts you to where you rightfully belong.

In Christ Jesus you come to the place of total dominion as citizens of God. Christ Jesus is the answer to every crisis in the world. Accept him, walk with him and overcome the prince of this world who is satan.

## Time Factor
(The Time Is Due)

*It is time to have faith in God*
*It is time to understand dominion*
*It is time to discover your place of dominion*
*It is time to take the very form of God*
*It is time to put your faith into action*
*It is time to develop the mindset of Jesus Christ for dominion*
*It is time to create a suitable and productive atmosphere*
*It is time to confess the word of God in every situation*
*It is time to give more attention to God's word*
*It is time to fulfill your birthright*
*It is time to align yourself with God through prayers.*


**"Obeying God's Word Alongside Prayers Will Propel You To Dominate..."**

# Other Books by the Author

- BEING DEBITED OR CREDITED
- DECIDING YOUR FUTURE
- DEALING WITH OFFENSES
- ACTS OF WISDOM
- ACTS OF FOOLISHNESS
- AND MANY OTHERS

For Further Information Please Contact
**Bright Boateng Ministries**
*P. O. Box Ks 17551*
*Adum, Kumasi – Ghana*
*West Africa*

*Email: Brightboateng@Gmail.Com*
*Call: +233 504 611 088*

# About the Author

Bright Boateng is a multi-gifted man of God to the body of Christ. He has the apostolic mandate to help people to discover the purpose of God for their lives.

He is the founder and president of Bright Boateng Ministries (BBM), based in Accra, Ghana. He is also the CEO of Bright Leadership Empowerment Consult (BLEC).

Bright Boateng has traveled extensively to many nations in Africa and beyond, to preach the Gospel of Jesus Christ with signs and wonders following.

His message centers on Jesus Christ, character, leadership and fulfilment of destiny.

Visit us on our website: www.brightboateng.org
🅕 Apostle Bright Boateng